D1593912

HANS URS VON BALTHASAR

The Theology of Henri de Lubac

HANS URS VON BALTHASAR

The Theology of Henri de Lubac

An Overview

A COMMUNIO BOOK

IGNATIUS PRESS   SAN FRANCISCO

Title of the German original:
Henri de Lubac: Sein organisches Lebenswerk
© 1976, Johannes Verlag Einsiedeln, Freiburg im Breisgau
Translated by Joseph Fessio, S.J., and Michael M. Waldstein

Conclusion translated from the French:
Le Cardinal de Lubac: L'Homme et son ouevre
by Hans Urs von Balthasar and Georges Chantraine, S.J.
© 1983, Ed. Lethielleux, Paris
Translated by Susan Clements

Pages 23–121 of the present work were first commissioned by *Thought* and published as "The Achievement
of Henri de Lubac" *Thought* 51 (March 1976), 6–49.
Reprinted with permission of the publisher c. 1976,
Fordham University Press, New York

Cover by Roxanne Mei Lum

© 1991 Ignatius Press, San Francisco
All rights reserved
ISBN 0-89870-350-6
Library of Congress catalogue number 91-71631
Printed in the United States of America

CONTENTS

ABBREVIATIONS

ExMed I, II	*Exégèse médiévale I* and *II*, 1959
ExMed III	*Exégèse médiévale III*, 1961
ExMed IV	*Exégèse médiévale IV*, 1964
F	*Le Fondement théologique des missions*, 1946
FCh	*La Foi chrétienne*, 1969
HA	*Le Drame de l'humanisme athée*, 1944 (quoted from pocketbook, 1963)
HE	*Histoire et esprit*, 1950
IM	*Images de l'abbé Monchanin*, 1967
M	*Méditation sur l'Eglise*, 1953
MS	*Le Mystère du surnaturel*, 1965
NP	*Nouveaux paradoxes*, 1955 (quoted from the double edition, 1959)
P	*Paradoxes*, 1946 (quoted from the double edition, *Paradoxes*, followed by *Nouveaux paradoxes*, 1959)
PCh	*Proudhon et le Christianisme*, 1945
Pic	*Pic de la Mirandole*, 1974
PME	*Paradoxe et mystère de l'Eglise*, 1967
PRel	*La Pensée religieuse du père Teilhard de Chardin*, 1962
PrT	*La Prière du père Teilhard de Chardin*, 1964
RB	*La Rencontre du Bouddhisme et de l'occident*, 1952
S	*Surnaturel*, 1946
TLI	*P. Teilhard de Chardin: Lettres intimes. . . ,* 1972
TMA	*Teilhard, Missionaire et apologiste*, 1966

PREFACE

I

This little work, which I wanted to hand to the friend and master on the occasion of his eightieth birthday, was complete in the form in which it had been commissioned first by the American journal *Thought* and then by the Belgian *Nouvelle revue théologique*, essentially in the form in which it appears here, when Father de Lubac placed in my hands and in the hands of some of his friends a manuscript of 150 large pages (furnished, as was to be expected, with many additional documents) in which he explains the meaning and fate of his books and places them in the context of his life, studies, encounters, friendships as well as the legendary condemnations and banishments prepared for him by his order and by the Church. These pages are so full of life and also so helpful for the correct understanding of his intentions that I cannot resist plucking a few blossoms from them to put into my own vase. De Lubac's glosses on his work are meandering, but they follow the chronological

The Preface has been translated by Michael Waldstein.

order; my glosses—which are intended to communicate no more than an elementary survey of the basic articulations of his work as a whole—are in a loose sense systematic. They do not want to put a straitjacket on de Lubac's work, which bursts out in all directions; they merely want to show that within the multiplicity of themes—often imposed on the author from the outside through academic duties, commissioned essays, lectures or orders of his superiors—an organic unity is at work.

He himself says it:

> Almost everything I have written sprang from unforeseeable circumstances, scattered, without technical preparation. In vain would one look for a true, personal philosophical or theological synthesis in the ensemble of such diverse publications, whether to criticize or approve it. And yet, in this many-colored fabric, occasioned by the conditions of the most various lectures, commissions, situations and calls, I nevertheless believe I can find some traces, a pattern that constitutes its unity.

He tells us even more. First, that together with some good friends—such as B. de Solages, Father Congar, Father Chenu, Mouroux, Chavasse, and others—he conceived the plan of a comprehensive theological work

> that would have been less systematic than the manuals but more saturated with tradition, integrating the valid elements in the results of modern exegesis, of patristics, liturgy, history, philosophical

reflection. . . . The lightning bolt of *Humani generis*
killed the project.

Then there is another important admission. Among
the numerous books of whose themes we hear that
were planned but never realized and for which ex-
tensive preparatory work and collection of materials
were completed, there is one that was for decades
particularly close to de Lubac's heart: a book about
the essence of Christian mysticism.

But the plan was too ambitious; nothing was realized.[1] I was never able to delimit the object clearly
enough. As early as 1956 I made the following
notes in order to situate the matter more clearly
—and I must admit that I am still standing at the
same point: "I believe my book on mysticism has
inspired me for a long time in everything I work
on; in its light I make my judgments and gain the
criteria for ordering my thoughts and ideas. But I
will never write this book. It goes in every respect
beyond my powers, physical, mental, and spiritual.
Its articulations stand clearly before my eyes. I see
the direction in which the problems must be dealt
with and in which their solution must be sought,
but I am unable to formulate this solution. Yet
this is sufficient for me to exclude at all times from
books I read and theories I find the points of view

[1] At least, following the wishes of Father A. Ravier, there
was the important introduction to a collection, *La Mystique et
les mystiques* (1965), in which he said, "I worked out some ideas
that, according to my original plan, should have been developed
in several volumes." In the light of the admission quoted below,
one will appreciate the importance of this synthesis.

that do not correspond to what I dimly perceive.
However, the final form always eludes me, the
form that would allow the work to realize itself."

De Lubac is not the only great author who understood and experienced all his completed works
as an approximation to an ever-unattained center.
This form gives the reader the chance of seeing
how seemingly disparate elements converge upon
a center and thus of grasping them in their secret
intention. In the case of de Lubac we will see,
in addition, that an objective fundamental insight
corresponds to the subjective admission quoted
above, namely, the role of an undeniably positive
dynamism in the knowing and willing of the creature that tends through all finite intraworldly reality
but also, through all the negations of "negative theology," toward a goal that cannot be reached "from
below" but is nevertheless necessary. Here we have
reached the center of de Lubac's principal problem,
as we will show in the sections about *Surnaturel* and
about *Creature and Paradox*.

II

The key-word "dynamism" offers an occasion to say
a little about those who have stimulated de Lubac's
thinking. Two names occur immediately, Blondel
and Maréchal. In fact, when de Lubac returned
from the war (with a wound that took its toll
throughout his life) and completed his philosophical and theological studies, these two were among

the great stimuli—one must count Rousselot among
them, because he taught de Lubac to see Thomas
anew. But de Lubac followed neither of them as
systematic theologians; he only adopted their fundamental élan, or rather he discovered this élan as
akin to his own nature and probably took from it
the courage to read out of the texts of Thomas
Aquinas what he saw in them with evidence: the
paradox of the spiritual creature that is ordained beyond itself by the innermost reality of its nature to
a goal that is unreachable for it and that can only
be given as a gift of grace. But while Maréchal,
threatened by censors, had to take refuge behind a
barbed-wire fence of distinctions and while Blondel, under the permanent terror of being put on the
Index, found himself ready for concessions in his
late work, de Lubac exposed himself to the attacks
of a tutiorist scholastic theology, armed with nothing but the historical and theological truth. Of the
three martyrs for truth, he was the most tortured,
far beyond the tortures endured by Blondel. A later
intimate friend, Étienne Gilson, confirmed him in
the midst of his afflictions with juicy and vigorous
letters. We cannot resist quoting a few sentences
from them.

> One fabricates a Thomism for the use of the
> schools, a sort of flat rationalism that fits every
> kind of deism—which is what most, at root, want
> to teach. The only salvation, by contrast, lies in go-
> ing back to Thomas himself, back behind John of
> St. Thomas, even behind Cajetan, whose famous

commentary is a successful "*corruptorium Sanctae Thomae*". . . . Thomas has been castrated by it.

And further, after reading *Surnaturel*,

> I can only agree with you, because what you say is true. It cannot be doubted. You are a theologian of great stature but likewise a humanist in the great tradition of humanist theologians. Humanist theologians usually do not love the scholastics, and they are almost always hated by the scholastics. Why? In part, it seems to me, because the latter understand only univocal propositions and those that seem to be univocal. The former, by contrast, are more interested in the truth that the proposition attempts to formulate and that always partly escapes it. Then the latter no longer understand; they become restless, and, because they cannot be certain that what escapes them is not false, they condemn it as a matter of principle, because that is more *secure*.

And, a little later,

> With regard to the essential question I find myself in agreement with you. *Le Mystère du surnaturel*, which I have just devoured, is simply perfect. I have the impression, not that the question is finished, because there are always people who confuse the issue, but that it should be finished. You have said everything one can say, especially the most important thing, namely, that in the end one must be silent. For we really stand before a mystery. . . . I see salvation only in a Thomasian philosophy, as you understand it, together with Augustine and

Bonaventure and the great Fathers of the East. All
of them are welcome, because despite certain unavoidable philosophical divergences they attempt
to communicate the "intellectus" of one and the
same faith.

Gilson's unqualified assent not only meant much to
his heavily pressed friend, it still means much today
to the reader, because it is the assent of the greatest
authority in the field of the history of philosophy.

De Lubac soon realized that his position moved
into a suspended middle in which he could not
practice any philosophy without its transcendence
into theology, but also no theology without its essential inner substructure of philosophy. This center has been the vital environment of his thought
from the beginning to the present, at the beginning in opposition to the modern dichotomy that
Cajetan had projected into Thomas, today in opposition to a new form of Christian schizophrenia
that yields so much to post-Kantian scientific rationalism and secularism (as "opening to the world")
that the only thing left for the sphere of faith is a
groundless fideism. Already in an early essay ("Sur
la philosophie chrétienne", 1936) de Lubac gives an
account of the polyvalence of such a middle, and he
demonstrates it in three contemporary examples:

> For Maritain there really is no Christian philo-
> sophy; what the philosophizing Christian receives
> from his faith is an external confirmation of his ra-
> tional reflection. For Gilson, who pays more care-
> ful attention to history, Christian revelation largely

brings about insights of reason, and thus there can be a philosophy that has its origin in Christianity; however, this philosophy stops being Christian and becomes purely rational when it becomes true philosophy. For Blondel, finally, who rejects the term "Christian philosophy", philosophy is not yet Christian because it excavates the emptiness that Christian revelation is destined to fill.

Beyond this, de Lubac thought there was a thinking illumined by the light of Christian faith, a thinking as the Church Fathers practiced it and for which he thought he could find points of departure in Gabriel Marcel.

In fact, the young scholastic nourished himself not only from the masters mentioned above, Irenaeus, Augustine, and Thomas, but also from Plotinus, Leibniz, and Malebranche. However, it was only after concluding his studies in theology, in 1929—that is, when he began to teach, first, fundamental theology and, shortly thereafter, history of religions at the Lyons *Faculté catholique*—that he began to read the Greek Fathers more closely. Twenty years later the book on Origen was published as a ripe fruit. But while the Fathers, first of all Origen, provided the formal example of an integration of faith and reason, Thomas, who stood on the boundary between antiquity and modernity, provided the critical formula for their inseparable unity: the suspended middle had to prove itself in his affirmations (which are indebted to the consensus of patristic theology) about the fundamental human "longing" that can be fulfilled only through grace. In *Surnaturel* de Lubac defends this suspended middle without any compromise against all attempts on the part of philosophers and theologians to bracket the other side. We will discuss this defense in detail below. A few things must be said here about its consequences for de Lubac.

Suspicions had surfaced even before *Surnaturel* (1946). *Surnaturel* had already been conceived during the confused years of German occupation and developed further in flight, first from the invading troops, then from the Gestapo. Father Garrigou-Lagrange spearheaded the catchword *Nouvelle théologie* (1946) against de Lubac and his friends; the Pope picked it up, at first with hesitation; *L'Osservatore Romano* repeated it; at first the Jesuit Father General Janssens stood honestly on de Lubac's side, but the more the attacks increased from all sides, the more diplomatic he became. Suspicious materials were dug out of other writings as well (*De la connaissance de Dieu*; *Corpus mysticum*; even the book on Origen). When *Humani generis* was published, a lightning bolt struck the school of theology in Lyons and de Lubac was branded as the principal scapegoat. The next ten years became a *via crucis* for him. He was deprived of permission to teach, expelled from Lyons and driven from place to place. His books were banned, removed from the libraries of the Society of Jesus and impounded from the market.

During all these years I was never questioned,
I did not have a single discussion with Roman
authorities about the main issues, neither with the
papal curia nor with the Society of Jesus. I was
never told what I was accused of; I was never asked
to provide something equivalent to a "retraction"
or declaration. Even in 1953, when I finally saw
the Father General, he continually evaded the issue,
both a discussion of the fundamental questions and
a discussion of particular facts.

It was a silent ostracism that drove the sensitive
man into complete isolation. The reversal came
very slowly: the Provincial, Father A. Ravier, insisted that de Lubac continue to work, even though
all his writings had to be sent to the Roman cen-
sor. Father de Finance obtained permission for the
publication of *Sur les chemins de Dieu*. Father Bea,
the Pope's confessor, insisted on handing some
of de Lubac's books to the Pope, and the Pope
thanked him with friendly words. Archbishop Mon-
tini gave him encouraging words (later, as Pope
Paul VI, he insisted that de Lubac speak about Teilhard de Chardin at the final session of the Thomist
Congress in the great hall of the Cancelleria), but
impenetrable clouds continued to shroud the moun-
tain for years—they were not even scattered when
de Lubac was elected a member of the *Institut de
France*. The course was finally turned when John
XXIII nominated him (together with Father Congar) as *consultor* for the preparatory theological com-
mission of the Council.

The years of the Council led to many contacts but also to much work; the postconciliar era brought many honors and many travels, including trips to North and South America. However, the one-sided development of the Society of Jesus in France—which was dominated by a small group of progressivists whose only Church Fathers had the names Marx, Freud, and especially Nietzsche—pushed the old master into the corner again. "What I wanted to offer as tasty nourishment and forward-looking power they now reject as a withered fruit or an uncomfortable burden." Although he is highly esteemed by many laypeople and priests, those who set the tone of the order consider him hopelessly outdated. And since he has found much to criticize in the theory and practice of postconciliar episcopal conferences, he is also not well liked in circles of the hierarchy.

III

It is well known that despite his great sensitivity the master did not allow himself to become bitter. He always found excuses and attenuating circumstances for what was done to him. He expressly stressed that his true opponents were not the Roman authorities but a group of integralist professors both in and outside the Society of Jesus. His unequivocal stance in favor of ecclesiastical authority, especially the papacy, shows that there was not a trace of anti-Roman sentiment in him. Much more painful than everything he had to endure in his beloved Society was his realization that the Society's authentic spirit began to wane in the years after the Council. He was never much concerned about his own books and influence, but much more about integrity of spirit. For this spirit would, in fact, be commissioned—today more so than ever—to penetrate the world with the salt of the gospel.

This is why de Lubac always attempted to act beyond himself. Two examples of this attempt must suffice as a conclusion to this preface. First of all, his important role in the foundation and guidance of the great series *Théologie*, over eighty volumes of which have been published since 1941—among them works of the highest intellectual and spiritual quality—all of which, one can safely say, are indebted and obliged to Henri de Lubac's genius, as his *Festschrift* (1963), published in three volumes in the same series, clearly shows. Secondly, his equally important participation in one of the most astonishing phenomena of today's Catholic Church, the *Sources chrétiennes*, for which he served as editor along with the unforgettable Father Daniélou and the untiring secretary, Father Claude Mondésert. Since 1940 they have succeeded in publishing more than 220 volumes, many of them in second and improved editions, a true fountain of life of Christian tradition from the Apostolic Fathers up to the high Middle Ages. In the face of the gigantic achievement of France (one should also mention Father Hamman's *Supplément* to Migne, the *Dictionnaire de spiritualité*, and the *Corpus christianorum* published in Belgium), the dissolution of German patristic studies (both the Berlin series and the Vienna series have been suspended!) must be considered particularly shameful. Germany may consider itself a leader in the field of exegesis and dogmatic theology, but it will only be and remain such if it continues to think and create out of the whole of Christian tradition as it did in the time of the Tübingen School. For this reason the figure of de Lubac must be familiar and dear to us even on this side of the Rhine, because it lives out an ideal that we should at least strive for, namely, the ideal of being a leader in the present because one knows the treasures of tradition as well as how to mint them into today's coinage; and because one is rooted in what is truly alive in Christianity in what is always for today and tomorrow because it shares in the spirit of the gospel.[2]

[2] In the spirit of ecclesial communion among the cultures of the world, the journal *Communio* began publication a few years ago. It was soon joined by a French edition edited mainly by young academics. Once again, the eighty-year-old de Lubac appeared as its true center by counseling, mediating, admonishing and helping, although he did not want to appear as the center. The French technical term for this role, which characterizes his entire attitude, is *effacé*.

I

PERSPECTIVE

Whoever stands before the forty or so volumes of Henri de Lubac's writings, with their more than 10,000 pages and hundreds of thousands of quotations—even disregarding the numerous articles and other smaller works—feels as though he is at the entrance to a primeval forest.[1] The themes could hardly be more diverse, and the gaze of the researcher glides seemingly without effort over the whole history of theology—and of thought itself. And yet in all this, not even the smallest details escape him—whether it be an obscure tractate of an early medieval author or a review in an equally obscure periodical. But to one who begins

The article "The Achievement of Henri de Lubac", originally written for *Thought* in German, has been translated by Joseph Fessio, S.J., and includes pp. 23–121 below.

[1] For a material overview, see Karl Neufeld-Michel Sales, *Bibliographie Henri de Lubac, S.J., 1925–1974*, 2. erganzte und verbesserte Auflage (Einsiedeln: Johannesverlag, 1975). Along with the chronological list of works, there is also a list of the major works with remarks of the author, of translations, and so on, as well as the most important discussions and analyses of the thought of Henri de Lubac.

to penetrate and become familiar with these major works, this seeming jungle reveals the order of an organic whole,[2] far from a textbook theology, that unfolds an eminently successful attempt to present the spirit of Catholic Christianity to contemporary man in such a way that he appears credible in himself and his historical development as well as in dialogue with the major forms of other interpretations of the world—and even feels confident in propos-

---

[2] The most important works cited here are: *Catholicisme* (1938); *Corpus mysticum* (1944); *Le Drame de l'humanisme athée* (1944); *Proudhon et le Christianisme* (1945); *Surnaturel* (1946); *Paradoxes* (1946); *Le Fondement théologique des missions* (1946); *Histoire et esprit* (1950); *Affrontements mystiques* (1950); *Aspects du Bouddhisme I* (1941); *La Rencontre du Bouddhisme et de l'occident* (1952); *Méditation sur l'Eglise* (1953); *Amida—Aspects du Bouddhisme II* (1955); *Nouveaux paradoxes* (1955); *Sur les chemins de Dieu* (1956); *Correspondance Blondel-Valensin* (3 volumes, 1957, 1965); *Exégèse médiévale I* and *II* (1959); *Exégèse médiévale III* (1961); *La Pensée religieuse du père Teilhard de Chardin* (1962); *Exégèse médiévale IV* (1964); *La Prière du père Teilhard de Chardin* (1964); *Augustinisme et théologie moderne* (1965); *Le Mystère du surnaturel* (1965); *Correspondance Blondel-Teilhard* (1965); *Teilhard, Missionnaire et apologiste* (1966); *Images de l'abbé Monchanin* (1967); *Paradoxe et mystère de l'Eglise* (1967); *L'Eternel féminin* (1968); *Athéisme et sens de l'homme* (1968); *Commentaire du préambule et du chapitre I de la constitution dogmatique "Dei Verbum"* (1968); *La Foi chrétienne* (1969); *L'Eglise dans la crise actuelle* (1969); *Correspondance Blondel-Wehrlé* (2 volumes, 1969); *Les Eglises particulières dans l'Eglise universelle* (1971); *P. Teilhard de Chardin: Lettres intimes . . .* (1972); *Pic de la Mirandole* (1974); See footnote 1 for works not mentioned here.

ing the unique complete ("catholic") solution to
the riddle of existence.

The height from which all is surveyed provides
a measure for the rising, soaring power that one
senses in the entire work—from the bold synthesis
in *Catholicisme* to the book on Pico by the almost
eighty-year-old theologian—an energy that carries
one along with it and that no willing reader can
escape. The same height explains the judgment in
matters of man's spirit, a judgment so free from
prejudice, a judgment that does not allow itself
to be unduly impressed even by strong intellectual movements or imposing personalities, knowing how to preserve a clear and objective distance,
however mild and circumspect the expression. Finally, this height is the reason for certain aspects, especially of the later works, that have been criticized
for their disillusionment and pessimism with regard to recent events in the Church; but these
aspects proceed simply from the fact that the author maintains firmly and without deviation his
original standard for genuine catholicity. It is out
of the question to think that he was in any way
embittered by the long period during which he
was proscribed within the Church because of *Surnaturel* (1946). In this instance he mirrors the experience of his friend Teilhard de Chardin, who
weathered the same quarrels and who, though not
unscathed, showed great courage. De Lubac surely
made Proudhon's remark his own: "From time

to time I must suffer a little and experience mis-
fortune; it sets me aright, reinvigorates me and does
me good."[3] And his citation of Teilhard is certainly
not gratuitous: "If you knew the bitterness of giving
in when one does not have the inner certitude that
it is right to give in, and when one fears, in spite
of everything, to be unfaithful to true courage and
true renunciation!"[4] But what follows will not trace
these inner afflictions that have been victoriously
overcome but rather the great spiritual options of
the master, options that determine his work and
choice of themes and in which only the will to serve
what has been objectively seen could have given
the impulse: "If there is any area where clarity and
precision of judgment is imperative, it is that of the
great spiritual decisions."[5]

This judgment, as a personal and totally committed one, is perceptible in all that de Lubac has
written—extending even to the choice of books he
reviewed—even and especially when in his prover-
bial modesty he almost always prefers to let a voice
from the great ecclesial tradition express what he
intends rather than raising his own voice. Already
in the foreword to *Catholicisme* one finds: "If the
quotations accumulate . . . , it is because we wished
to proceed as impersonally as possible, drawing especially on the too-little utilized treasures of the

[3] PCh 56.
[4] PrT 82.
[5] RB 282.

Fathers of the Church."[6] And yet the author's opinion can be easily discerned in the web of quotations —especially when one pays close attention to the critiques and corrections of the passages cited—just as the intention of a playwright can be heard in the chorus of his actors' voices.

If we attempt to trace de Lubac's fundamental options, a glance at his bibliography can provide us with an initial insight: the astounding fact that his most important themes emerge and ripen much earlier than the finished books would lead us to suspect. He was already concerned with mysticism in 1926, while the now-classical article on mysticism appeared in 1965. The studies leading up to *Surnaturel* (1946) were begun in 1931; the chapters of what will later be a book grow together concentrically,[7] and this mode of origin is at times still perceptible. What is more important, the primary intuitions at the origin of the later works are all present together at a chronologically early period. This demonstrates that they are also objectively only aspects of an integral vision and decision, although one that is richly articulated. This is the starting point for the elaboration of material that is often immensely rich and wide-ranging; de Lubac could say, as Hegel did: "I know just about all of what is great and glorious in the ancients and

[6] C xiii.

[7] This is demonstrated in greater detail for *Catholicisme* and *Surnaturel* in the bibliography of Neufeld-Sales, 62–65.

moderns; and one should and can know it."[8] At the beginning of his prodigious *Exégèse médiévale*, he tells us at least: "We have read as many texts as possible."[9] Nor was any change of perspective necessary for the first intuition.

Going a step further, we will not go wrong in referring to de Lubac's interest as being primarily theological. The major themes confirm this repeatedly. But it would be premature on their account to reproach him, as has been done, for any deficiency in philosophy. This is contradicted not only by his serious and careful study of the whole of French philosophy in his own works[10] and by his learned commentary on Blondel's correspondence but above all by his conception of "Catholicism" as "*the* religion"[11]—a conception that presupposes a profound understanding not only of the other world religions but also of the world systems and philosophies inseparably bound up with them. Finally, we see that deeply meditated philosophical options clearly underlie his works.

His first major work, *Catholicisme*, which sets the style and orientation for all that will follow, reveals the fundamental decision as a decision for fullness, totality, and the widest possible horizon—it is precisely the power of inclusion that becomes the chief

[8] *Ästhetik*, 2d ed. (Bassenge, 1965), II 568.
[9] ExMed I 20.
[10] See especially Ch, but also PCh.
[11] C 256.

criterion of truth—so that, negatively, it becomes a major concern of his to point out where the entire tradition, and in particular the ecclesial and theological tradition, has become narrow or rigid, often with immensely destructive consequences. With respect to "Western man's turning away from his Christian origins", "an immense drift" is spoken of.[12] "Modern humanism is constructed upon a resentment and begins with a fundamental option: that of *anti-theism*."[13] This means, according to Proudhon: "There should be no illusions about it; Europe is tired of order and thought; it is entering a period of brutal power, of contempt of principle, of intoxication."[14] And Proudhon concludes (as does de Lubac): "One must go back to the sources and seek the divine."[15] In the ecclesial-theological domain, the evident as well as the hidden catastrophes always occur where, for reasons of apologetics, polemics, or an apparent logic, one abandons a total, catholic standpoint for the sake of a particular standpoint, an *anti*-position. Outstanding examples: the abandoning of the concrete, salvation-historical thought of the Fathers and high scholasticism in favor of a rationalistic thought that has led to the separation in anthropology between (self-contained) natural finality and

[12] HA 5.
[13] HA 20.
[14] PCh 10.
[15] PCh 308.

supernatural orientation (the starting point for *Sur-naturel*); or the giving up of a genuinely theological symbolic thinking in the case of the Eucharist, which was the occasion for a one-sided emphasis upon the real presence and thus for the disintegration of the Church-Eucharist mystery (the starting point for *Corpus mysticum*); not to mention the "combined influence of Aristotelian logic and Roman law upon the development of medieval theology, especially upon the treatise on the Church";[16] the "individualistic aberrations of theology" without which "the Marxist-Leninist error would perhaps never have arisen or would not have spread so disastrously";[17] the 'anti'-positions of the Counter-Reformation, which have resulted in a professional, convulsive constriction in theology.[18]

One might think that de Lubac would call upon great allies to take up the defense against such devastating contractions of theology,[19] that he would perhaps write monographs on Bonaventure, Nicholas of Cusa, Pascal, Moehler, Newman, and others. He knows these allies thoroughly and quotes them appropriately in their place. But it is characteristic of him to choose other representatives of universal thought, namely, the great

[16] C 265, 271f.

[17] C 266–67.

[18] C 273.

[19] For in fact "humanity must be understood from its summits". C 257f.

among the vanquished who have fallen because of
the machinations of smaller minds or of a narrow
Catholicism that is politically rather than spiritually
minded. Thinkers, nevertheless, who either had in
fact or ought to have had a profound effect. The
outstanding example here is Origen, to whom not
only a very central work (*Histoire et esprit*) and
numerous introductions to his works (in *Sources
chrétiennes*) are dedicated but whose legends, along
with the adventuresome history of the ramifications
of his thought, have been pursued through the centuries;[20] next in importance is the example of Teilhard de Chardin, who came perilously close to con-
demnation by the Church. It was due, after all, to
the numerous publications of de Lubac that he was
spared that fate. But *Corpus mysticum* is also a work
of rehabilitation of those who have unjustly found
themselves under the wheels (Amalarius, among
others); the history of medieval exegesis ends in a
well-documented justification of Erasmus against
the many who distorted his more profound intentions; it is here that the almost oversized apology of Pico della Mirandola branches off, as he is
defended from all sides against historically senseless and biased judgments by famous scholars of
the history of ideas and resituated in the historical
setting that belongs to him. Once again we are
indebted to de Lubac's extraordinary knowledge

[20] ExMed I 221–304, and frequently.

of the tradition. A perhaps even more important work on Fénelon, the last major representative of a great spirituality and a man violently rendered powerless, was planned. De Lubac passed on the papers he had collected for this to a fellow Jesuit working on Fénelon. The commentaries on Blondel's letters belong here. They are a memorial to the greatest Catholic philosopher of modern France, a man tortured for decades to the point of blood by reactionary theologians. And one of de Lubac's unusual books should be included here: *Proudhon et le Christianisme*, a work that treats its central figure with the necessary critical distance and yet portrays him, in spite of his unruliness, as one who justifiably reacted against an intolerably narrow, reactionary, traditionalist Catholicism.

Proudhon holds a mirror before a disfigured Church. He not only takes a position against Feuerbach and Strauss,[21] against the Saint-Simonists,[22] against a socialized gospel,[23] but above all against a Church fundamentally bound up with riches and luxury;[24] a Church that considers throne and altar inseparable,[25] that preaches almsgiving instead of social justice (de Lubac multiplies horrifying ex-

[21] PCh 139f.
[22] PCh 223.
[23] PCh 20.
[24] PCh 85, 104f.
[25] PCh 197.

amples),[26] that degrades the living God to a mere
"providence",[27] and that, instead of serious theology,[28] now espouses only the theory of traditional-
ism.[29] It is no wonder that Proudhon writes "Rev-
olution and Justice" on his banner instead and
struggles for the concept of a God who leaves
man the dignity of his freedom.[30] De Lubac is not
sparing in his criticism of his champion—of his character as well as of his ideas—but neither does he
begrudge him sympathy when he treats the "Proud-
honian virtues",[31] and, in the final race, he lets him
win out against Marx.[32] Proudhon bows beneath
the highest authority of an immanent ethical idea
(although he divinizes it),[33] while Marxist man cre-
ates himself and this idea as well.

The example is instructive in that it shows that
de Lubac never paints in black and white, one-
sidedly. When, in the question of a "natura pura"
(and its consequences, which lead all the way to
modern secularism[34]), he raises serious objec-

[26] PCh 211ff.
[27] PCh 194ff.
[28] PCh 106f.
[29] PCh 273ff.
[30] PCh 190; the whole idea of the antinomian equilibrium, the
rhythm of opposites, the mutual intensification, is also applied
to God and man: PCh 151–77.
[31] PCh 53–80.
[32] PCh 314.
[33] PCh 296–301.
[34] AthS 102–3.

tions against Cajetan's interpretation of Thomas and against Suarez, he does not do so without pointing out the earlier stages of their idea in other authors and in the general spirit of the time, which was moving in this direction. He is more stringent with modern scholars—as in the misinterpretations of Pico by thinkers such as Ernst Cassirer or Lucien Febvre (to name only protagonists of a legion of others)—because their scientific attitude ought to have prevented them from wearing such blinders and because he cannot forgive them their ignorance of the patristic and medieval tradition.

II

CATHOLICISME

With what has been said up to now, we are prepared to cross the threshold and consider the content of de Lubac's work. At the beginning stands the programmatic *Catholicisme* (1938), a work that was intended to be and actually became a major breakthrough. The major works that followed grew from its individual chapters much like branches from a trunk. Because of this work's seminal importance, it is necessary to spend some time with it here.

The work is divided into three sections. The first two indicate the two major characteristics of Catholicism: (1) the "social" (let us say in clarification: the universal solidarity in what concerns the salvation of man); and (2) the "historical" (the significance of time and history). The third section is complementary: it shows first the relevance of what has been considered (the tenth chapter, "The Present Situation", could stand as an introduction to the whole book), then the necessary dialectic between person and community (eleventh chapter), between immanent and transcendent salvation.

The first section develops the idea of total solidarity in four steps (each a chapter): (1) Since the God of creation and the God of redemption are one and the same, since mankind as created forms a unity as well, God's intention in the redemption of the world in Christ can once again intend mankind only as a whole. (This position stands against any Jansenistic restriction of redemption to the "elect", as well as every form of individualism in the matter of salvation. If the Church had consistently avoided this stance, Marxism would probably have been superfluous.)[1] Here, as in all the succeeding chapters, a superabundance of texts from the great tradition is brought to bear in confirmation. (2) The Church founded by Christ can be ordered only to this totality of redemption. She continues the work of unifying a mankind cut to pieces by sin and egoism; she touches the whole of man; she must be at the same time visible-corporeal and invisible-spiritual as he is; she is the "Sacrament of Christ in the world".[2] This ordination to solidarity is especially clear in her sacraments. Baptism is incorporation into the people of God; confession is always reconciliation with this holy people as well as with God; the Eucharist above all is the mystery of the deepest union with the brothers. (Only after the accent had been displaced from the social aspect

[1] C 274.
[2] C 50.

to that of the real presence did individualistic eucharistic piety win a handhold. This is the point of departure for the problematic of *Corpus mysticum* [1944].) Christ's body of flesh was called by the Fathers the "*soma typicon*", which, through his "mystical body" (*corpus mysticum*), the Eucharist, built up his true body, the Church.[3] Liturgical texts corroborate these expressions. (4) The world's redemption and the earthly Church have as their goal eternal life, which is portrayed in Scripture and tradition as communion in the trinitarian God: the heavenly Jerusalem. What is of lasting significance in Origen's conception—which found such a strong echo throughout history (and finally had to be repudiated)—that Christ and the blessed attain their ultimate beatitude only when the entire "Body of Christ", the redeemed creation, is gathered together in the transfiguration, is given its due place.[4]

The second section unfolds the historical dimension in five steps. Insofar as God in Jesus Christ enters into the movement of history, the direction of this history's flow holds a meaning. (1) This is in contrast to all nonbiblical religions, which can extract no salvific meaning from history and can therefore essentially offer religion only as "an individualistic doctrine of evasion."[5] (Two series of works take their point of departure here: first, the

[3] C 74.
[4] C 93-100.
[5] C 107.

dialogue with Buddhism; then the works in defense of Teilhard de Chardin, which demonstrate that his evolutionism and his turning toward the omega of history are essentially biblical and traditional.)[6] (2) But God's entrance into history divides it also as salvation history into great periods; promise and fulfillment, Old Covenant-New Covenant. According to Paul, they are related to each other as "letter" and "spirit". The transcendence of the latter over the former forms the central event of Christianity that remains continuously present at every moment. This transcendence therefore provides the key for the interpretation of Holy Scripture. (This is the point of departure for all the works on theological exegesis: from the book on Origen, *Histoire et esprit*, 1950—the two words stand already as the heading of a subsection in *Catholicisme*, pp. 135ff.—to the mammoth *Exégèse médiévale*, 1959–1964, and, as a sort of postlude, *Pic de la Mirandole*, 1974.) (3) In the following seventh chapter, the problematic of the second chapter returns: how can a circumscribed and limited historical form, the

[6] The theme of the maturation of the world through history can be documented from Irenaeus to Teilhard de Chardin. A confrontation with the Iranian religion, which supposedly also thinks historically, reveals the opposition: the historical character of Mazdaism is a secondary layer superimposed upon a cosmological myth; while in Israel, the historical Covenant is and remains the foundation for all the cosmological outgrowths of faith in Yahweh.

Catholic Church, be ordered to the salvation of the entire world? In what sense is she "necessary for salvation"? Grace can also work outside of her; why not speak therefore of an "implicit Christianity" in "anonymity" (long before K. Rahner) for non-Christians?[7] De Lubac's solution is both new and subtle, growing out of his principle of history's meaningful direction. As with the Old Covenant, so all the religious efforts of man have contributed in their own way and at their stage of development to provide the basis of the coming consummation. They must, of course, give up their claims to be "objective systems" offering something whole and complete,[8] but insofar as the pre-Christian efforts

> were indispensable for the building up of Christ's body, "unbelievers" must profit in their own way from the vital exchanges within this body. By an extension of the dogma of the communion of saints, it seems right to think that although they themselves lack the normal conditions for salvation, they will be able nevertheless to obtain this salvation by virtue of the mysterious bonds that unite them to believers. . . . What is insufficient can be sufficient because the "more" exists to supply what is lacking.[9]

[7] C 183.

[8] C 185. In other words, there is no "anonymous Christianity" but at best "anonymous Christians" in virtue of the grace that can produce effects even in deficient systems.

[9] C 194.

More profoundly: whatever contributes to the breakthrough of Christ is not mere "material" but human persons who participate in the success of their labors, even when this success remains transcendent to their efforts. Any mission to a given people intends and extends to that people's ancestors as well.[10] This theory, supported as always by patristic texts, in no way makes the Church's mission superfluous but rather makes it more urgent. (The brief study on *The Theological Foundation of the Missions* [1946] would be published shortly after this.) Since the transition from the state of promise to that of fulfillment is obligatory, so too is the mission of the Church (as progressive radiation of salvation into the consciousness of mankind) and the Christian's responsibility for the world: the Christian has a duty of "collaboration" rather than "evasion".[11] It will be necessary to recall this chapter when we look for something on the order of a summarizing formula for de Lubac's philosophical-theological world vision. (4) But a question remains, arising from the insertion of Christ and the Church in time: Why did the fulfillment come so late? What is the purpose of the apparently endless prehistory? The answer (in chapter 8) is twofold. It points back to the already-mentioned idea of the historical maturation of humanity toward free-

[10] C 195.
[11] C 200.

dom, its "habituation" (Irenaeus) to the law of the Logos, and exploits the value of the Pauline-patristic theme of the divine pedagogy, even giving it a universal-historical significance that anticipates Teilhard's vision. In this way the experience of mankind can be accented both positively and negatively (the experience of one's own weakness): all historical progress remains ambiguous. But a new theme arises from this: that of the infallible predestination of the Church throughout her entire prehistory and history. "The Church is predestined and, in her, all of man and the entire universe."[12] This predestination lets Paul break out into the cry of joy, "*O Altitudo!*", at the end of his theology of history (Romans 11). In whatever way the destiny of the individual may remain in ultimate uncertainty, "one thing is certain: the Church will not enter into the kingdom of God mutilated on the last day."[13] In a concluding remark, de Lubac protects himself against any identification of this doctrine with that of the apocatastasis. But there is no doubt that this chapter anticipates Barth's famous doctrine of predestination (K.D. II, 2), in which he inserts a weighty chapter on the election of the Church between the election of Christ and the election of the individual. Again, it becomes clear (beginning from Romans 11) that the preliminary

[12] C 233f.
[13] C 238.

stage—recapitulated in Israel—will be taken up into the definitive stage: the concluding transcendence does not leave behind what has made it possible but brings it to its own completion, both preserving and "elevating" it. (5) In the last (ninth) chapter of the second section, entitled "*Catholicisme*", this is brought into sharper focus in its application to the Church, which must, in her expanding movement, conform the world to herself—"transforming" it![14] For the "work of the Creator, however much it may be ruined by man, remains the natural and necessary preparation for the work of the Redeemer." "Christianity has transformed the ancient world by absorbing it into itself. . . . These roots are all the more necessary as the transcendence is more elevated. 'Supernatural' does not at all mean 'superficial'."[15] The "method of immanence is the one most deeply rooted in the tradition."[16] Therefore, every form of missiological pessimism—"Islam, India, Communism cannot be converted"—is really lack of faith.

After the tenth chapter, which is actually the introduction to the whole book, since it develops the program of a theology free from constrictions and the self-limitations of every "anti"-theology, strong and bold enough to bear the "most extreme

[14] C 243.
[15] C 244.
[16] C 25.

tension" without turning into Hegelianism,[17] the third section turns, in two concluding chapters, to the perduring dialectics of person-community (chapter 11) and immanence-transcendence (chapter 12). By maintaining these tensions, and even carrying them through to their ultimate consequences, Catholicism has a superior vantage point from which it can engage in the dialogue with Buddhism, on the one hand, and Communism on the other. "The most perfect and enjoyable existence from the social point of view would be the most inhuman if it did not serve the interior (personal) life; just as the latter would remain no more than mystification were it to turn back upon itself in refined egoism."[18] And so *Catholicisme* has led us, on the one hand, to this double dialogue with these world-historical partners and, on the other hand, to the task of constructing out of the origins (that always lie open to us), yet without historicism,[19] a theology of true synthesis.

---

[17] C 263ff. The problem of *Surnaturel* (C 270f.), on the one hand, that of *Corpus mysticum* (C 275f.), on the other, are mentioned as examples of a tension to be mastered.

[18] C 316.

[19] C 326: "For it is just as unsatisfactory to copy Christian antiquity as it would be to imitate the Middle Ages." See also: "*Pour une renaissance 'catholique'*" in *Explication chrétienne de notre temps* (Paris: Orante, 1942), 23ff.

THE TWO "ATHEISMS"

The Church not only has the obligation of being missionary, but mission is her proper essence; the short treatise *The Theological Foundation of the Missions* (1946) makes the point again in its central argument. Already in Israel, the suffering, redeeming servant of God is at the same time the one who proclaims the Law of Yahweh to all peoples.[1] But there is a contradiction in the Old Covenant that resists this synthesis: for Israel is a people "according to the flesh" and can only fulfill its universal mission through the artificial solution of proselytism.[2] It is only the passage to the definitive Covenant through Christ that frees Israel from the contradiction; now Catholicity is at the same time given in principle but also demanded in principle; it is "not properly speaking a thing, something objectively given, in any case no mere empirical fact; the Church is Catholic because, understanding herself to be universal *de jure*, she desires also to become so *de facto*."[3] Catholicity is "dynamic" and therefore

[1] F 23.
[2] F 25ff.
[3] F 30.

"missionary".[4] And if she also knows that the light of the Logos and the grace of Christ "is at work everywhere under a thousand anonymous forms",[5] still the Church is interiorly a part of this working of God in the world; "if she did not seek to be everywhere, she would be nowhere."[6]

From the very beginning, de Lubac recognized the two essential front lines of missionary dialogue and carried on this dialogue simultaneously, so to speak; his articles, however, which from 1972 on prepared for his works on modern atheism (1944/1945), preceded the articles that (from 1937 on, but more especially from 1950) introduced the works on Buddhism (1951/1952/1955). The first theme was a burning personal concern of the author; the second was a task given him more or less unexpectedly by his dean at the theological faculty of Lyons.[7] But this theme too must have appealed to him, for "with the exception of the unique Fact in which we adore the vestige and the very Presence of God, Buddhism is without doubt the greatest spiritual fact in the history of man."[8]

[4] F 32.
[5] F 35.
[6] F 41.
[7] AB I 7.
[8] AB I 8.

Western Atheism

The dialogue with modern atheism takes place in three works: *Le Drame de l'humanisme athée* (1944), *Proudhon et le Christianisme* (1945), *Athéisme et sens de l'homme* (in connection with *Gaudium et spes* [1968]). There has already been a short exposition of *Proudhon*; because of the eccentricity of its hero, the book remains something of a stepchild among de Lubac's works. The third book is short and is presented as an interpretation of the Council's pastoral constitution, in which "the section on atheism appears as the *punctum saliens* of the whole constitution."[9] In addressing itself vigorously to those within the Church, that is, against every form of an "atheistic hermeneutics of Christianity",[10] against the identification, for example, of the mystical night of a John of the Cross with the nights of a Nietzsche, against the death-of-God theology, the "fever for demythologization", purely "functional thought" that holds all ontology to be obsolete and "flirts with its own unbelief" or with Tillich sees doubt as belonging to faith,[11] in proclaiming "the hour of real spiritual confrontation" and ridiculing those who "want to recognize only verbal distinctions between believers and unbe-

[9] AthS 13.
[10] AthS 23ff.
[11] AthS 18f., 38f., 77–83.

lievers",[12] it already belongs essentially to de Lubac's later period, which we will characterize farther on. It points out forcefully that the real twilight of the gods has already begun with the gospel,[13] that (in continuation of the final chapter of *Catholicisme*) transcendence and immanence always condition each other mutually (a fact that constitutes the whole structure of *Gaudium et spes*),[14] that a purely immanent notion of culture remains an inner contradiction—more and more freedom and at the same time more and more organization,[15] "increasing rationality and increasing absurdity"[16]—and that it is only the Christian with his hope beyond failure[17] and death[18] who can give to world history its meaning and direction.[19]

And so the first of these three books remains the central work, supplemented by the important study of Nietzsche in *Affrontements mystiques* (1950). *Le Drame* is a book that is externally a collection of articles loosely gathered together but internally a powerfully constructed work. There are three

[12] AthS 73, 72.
[13] AthS 55.
[14] AthS 93ff.
[15] AthS 61.
[16] AthS 111.
[17] AthS 131.
[18] AthS 58.
[19] The enquiry ends in the question of how far *Gaudium et spes* was able to handle the depth of the dilemma between Christian transcendence and the formation of a culture.

parts. (1) Feuerbach—(Marx)—Nietzsche—Kierkegaard: the tragic prophecy of atheism; (2) Comte:
the solemn (and grotesque) inauguration of the new
religion of humanity, presented as being beyond
atheism; (3) the anti-atheistic prophet Dostoevsky,
his depth, his ambiguity and eventual emergence
into unambiguous clarity. The author's heart is in
sympathy with Nietzsche's (and Kierkegaard's) inner struggle. He maintains a devastating objectivity
in face of Comte's petrified solemnity, wholly in
contrast to his sketch of Proudhon. In de Lubac's
entire work there is only one other rejection as radical as this: that of Joachim of Flore,[20] for the other
comparable position against Denis the Areopagite
is much more nuanced.

Feuerbach appears as the one who immediately
triggers the fateful process: "The conjunction of
French socialism, English economic theory and
German metaphysics could have produced something totally different from Marxism if Marx had
not found a master in Feuerbach."[21] But even
Nietzsche is more indebted to Marx than he ad-
mits: through the intermediaries Schopenhauer and
Wagner.[22] For him also, God can only live in man's
consciousness—and die there in order to be replaced
by the liberated and expanded human consciousness. This consciousness exalts itself in its expecta-

[20] ExMed III 437–558.
[21] HA 33.
[22] HA 35.

tion of the Superman and at the same time deepens itself in 1881 through the revelation of the eternal return, strengthened in 1882 by Zarathustra's vision. How was it possible for the contradictions between these two thoughts to remain hidden to Nietzsche? How was it possible for the frightening idea of the return to appear to him as the highest beatitude? The solution de Lubac proposes in his "*Nietzsche mystique*" is credible:

> He can be driven passively, caught up in the enormous, despairing cyclical movement, but he can also share in the controlling power that thus moves the universe; he can suffer the iron law of universal determinism, but he can also freely be the law itself; he can love this fatality to the point of identification with it: "*Amor Fati. Ego Fatum.*"[23]

Becoming and being coincide. Whoever stands on the side of becoming will be overpowered by it: nihilism; but whoever can become one with being experiences divine beatitude. Since the vision of Rapallo, Nietzsche knows that this has happened to him, that he is the Superman, "participating in *Natura naturans*".[24] And so he has succeeded, as he desired, in establishing a "European Buddhism"; here, too, Samsara and Nirvana coincide.[25] Like the enlightened disciple of Buddha, he is "neither in a Nirvana separated from the world nor

[23] AfM 158–59.
[24] AfM 162.
[25] AfM 163.

any longer imprisoned in Samsara."[26] This is the atheistic substitute for the dead Christian God—Nietzsche always measures himself secretly against Jesus and his effect upon the world—a substitute that, even experientially, bursts open human consciousness: "I must persevere in my dream if I am not to perish"; "The moment in which I gave birth to the eternal return is immortal, and I carry the burden of the eternal return out of love for this moment." Suicide was here a "relatively pleasant thought"; madness overtook him.

We may pass over the spiritual duel between Nietzsche and Kierkegaard; let it be merely noted that de Lubac sees the position of Socrates as central for both of them; for Nietzsche it is the prelude to decadence; for Kierkegaard it is the prefiguring shadow of Christ, almost his "Old Covenant". Nevertheless, even if Kierkegaard, as moralist and Christian, "was ultimately in the right against Hegel" the question remains: "Does he recognize what a 'converted' Hegelianism—like all great human thought—could contribute to an authentic understanding of faith?"[27] The duel between Nietzsche and Dostoevsky is more dramatic—approaching the exchange of rapiers as in Hamlet. Let us first take note here of a trait that holds for all de Lubac's portraits in the history of thought. He prepares by

[26] AfM 165.
[27] HA 71ff., 87.

reading as exhaustively as possible not only the major works but the other works as well. He draws information from journals, letters, and notes, from everything that touches on the figure in question, all the accessible biographies and essays. This detailed knowledge can then give rise to a very differentiated evaluation. While the author first seems enthralled by the person he is considering, he then takes a step back. The last appraisal is made in unbiased objectivity. Dostoevsky is concerned with "atheism", as his five-volume major work was to have been called.[28] Thus originate *The Idiot*, *The Devils*, "The Grand Inquisitor". Atheism is reduced *ad absurdum* in the dialectic of Raskolnikov ("Napoleon or a scoundrel"), of Kirillov (who kills himself in order to kill death), of Zhigalov ("starting from unlimited freedom, I have arrived at unlimited despotism"), of Ivan Karamazov (the inquisitor as high priest of humanity, who sacrifices himself and those like him for the happiness of man). But the real battle is waged between Kirillov and Myshkin (the "Idiot"). Both know Dostoevsky's "experience of eternity", of that exalted moment of happiness before the epileptic fit, but they interpret it in opposite ways. For the latter, it is the awareness of being like God, of the "man-God"; for the former, it is a type of support for Christian faith.[29] De Lubac refuses, however,

[28] HA 236, 365–66.
[29] HA 291–329.

as did Guardini, Thurneyson, and Zander, among others, to see in Myshkin a cryptic symbol for Jesus. He distances himself from Dostoevsky's exuberant "love of the great mother, the moist earth", and of the messianic Russian people. He pursues the double theme in Dostoevsky's work, the shifting transitions between psychology and metaphysics, all that is "ambiguous",[30] and thus prevented from entering into the properly Christian sphere. Only a few scenes are for him a clear conquest: the final scene with Raskolnikov, Aliosha. . . .

At the center, between the duels of the prophets, de Lubac places the finished portrait—elaborated with grim coolness—of the high priest of a godless humanity, Auguste Comte. The culmination of a sociocracy that has completely swallowed up all theology and philosophy, all fact-transcending thought. The putting to death of the essential question. The law of the three stages (theology-metaphysics-positivism) strangely surpassing itself to become an apology of the first stage, as fetishism.[31] The solidification of Church discipline into a despotic authority of scholars as the priestly caste, of bankers as those really in control of man's destiny, and next to them a working proletariat,[32] the rejection of every form of democracy. There is still much in this grotesque image—of a total state as a congeal-

[30] HA 317.
[31] HA 127f., 187.
[32] HA 212.

ing and secularization of the Catholic Church—that can be held before us today, like a mirror, after more than a hundred years.

Eastern Atheism

The dialogue with the second, "vertical" atheism—Buddhism—is managed no less intensely and carefully. *Aspects du Bouddhisme* (1951) poses the major question: What is the relation between selfless love in Buddhism and *caritas* in Christianity? (The other contributions are more individual studies.) *La Rencontre du Bouddhisme et de l'occident* (1952) recounts the history of Europe's encounter with the spiritual phenomenon, the innumerable misunderstandings and hesitations, the obscuring of real issues, to such an extent that only recently an objective judgment has become possible. *Amida—Aspects du Bouddhisme II* (1955) meticulously traces the genesis of this Eastern religion that stands closest to the Christian concept of grace.[33]

Despite its abundant material, drawn from the history of thought extending from the Middle Ages until today, the *Rencontre* does not make a very great theological contribution. It portrays—after the

[33] Since de Lubac is not an orientalist by specialty, he used all the available translations and secondary sources (primarily in the library of the Musée Guimet). He presents his work as "the first monograph in the French language and not able to make any claims to critical erudition." Am 8.

vague prelude in antiquity—the insights of the four-
teenth-century travellers, the obscuring of these insights and the new approach of the missionaries,
their misunderstandings, and, for the most part,
unfavorable judgments. The encounter takes on
seriousness with the scientific research of language
and texts (especially by Burnouf, whose positivism,
however, impedes a deeper understanding).[34] Then
come the subsequent controversies, in part biased
by current fashion, the judgments from the Christian side, inhibited and falsified by a traditionalist
theology,[35] the over-hasty syntheses of Eastern and
Western mysticism (Ghénon, Schuon, more differentiated with A. Schweitzer, Scheler, R. Otto,[36]
among others), until finally—today—the time has become ripe for a really objective evaluation. But, "for
the wider, so-called cultivated public, Buddhism remains a *terra incognita*."[37] In the last analysis, three basic positions can be taken with regard to Buddhism:
(1) a humanistic position that exposes without bias
the human values (for example, Silvain Levi, Mal-
raux, already Michelet); (2) a proselytizing position
(Kayserling, A. Huxley, among others[38]); (3) finally,
the Christian position, which, while recognizing

[34] RB 132ff.

[35] RB 184ff.

[36] A confrontation with Paul Deussen is lacking.

[37] RB 261.

[38] The paradoxical affinity with Nietzsche is mentioned again
here: RB 274ff.

all that is positive (Soloviev), "can only reject" the system, since "its mysticism, the purest and most coherent there is, leaves no room at all for the living God." It is an "atheism", which explains why Schopenhauer, who wanted to demolish "the absurd and revolting theism" of the Bible, valued it so highly.[39]

Aspects I and *Amida* examine more closely the grounds for this ultimately negative judgment. *Aspects I* shows that in Buddhism love is based on "*ahimsa*" (nonviolence, nonresistance) and develops in the fundamental attitudes of "*matri*" (benevolence, kindness), "*dana*" (gift, physical and spiritual willingness to help), and "*karuna*" (sympathy).[40] It is above all the Greater Vehicle that glorifies these virtues, which are to be exercised in perfect selflessness and universality, without expecting any reward. De Lubac cites extremely impressive texts. Then the theological reflection begins. Since the idealistic monism that lies at the bottom of Buddhism renders impossible the existence of a true Thou who could be loved as such, Buddhistic love remains ultimately without an object. Objects only exist for the uninitiated.[41] Everything is dreamlike, incompatible with a genuine incarnation; love remains a preliminary stage because ultimately there is

[39] RB 278–79.
[40] These virtues are for the most part already known in India's pre-Buddhic systems.
[41] AB I 36ff., 46.

no opposition of persons. "All the insufficiency—all the falsity—of the Buddhist religion stems primarily from this."[42] The radical inclination away from reality leads finally to an ultimate identification of Samsara and Nirvana,[43] as was already mentioned in Nietzsche's regard. "Salvation, says Asanga, is the destruction of a mere prejudice; there is no one who is saved."[44]

Amida leads to exactly the same result by more roundabout paths. The demonstration of the mystical origin of the figure of Amida and its "heaven", its repression of other competing figures or its fusion with them, its begetting of a feminine figure out of itself, who becomes in Japan the famous Kwannon,[45] lets the religion that has roots already in India, is developed in China and is still evolving vigorously in Japan—the religion of a "gracious", "descending" God and a vow of total dedication to him whereby all guilt is forgiven the believer —appear as lacking any historical foundation. The

[42] AB I 53. Of the studies that follow, the one on the *Trikayu*, the doctrine of the three bodies in Buddhism and (Alexandrian) Christianity may be mentioned. After noting the striking parallels (see already: *Textes aléxandrins et bouddhiques*, 27, RSR, 1937), the same diagnosis is again reached: in Christianity, everything is predominantly realistic (all the way to the resurrection of the body); in Buddhism, every differentiation remains purely phenomenal.

[43] AB I 140.
[44] AB I 141.
[45] Am 127ff.

tradition, which is branching off into ever more numerous sects, especially in Japan, cannot be traced
here. An influence of (Nestorian) Christianity is
dismissed as very improbable; Iranian inspiration is
more likely,[46] but also Vedic; influences from the
bhakti religion may have played a role. The sim-
ilarity between the Amida-vow and the faith attitude (of apparently Lutheran stamp), though at first
glance astonishing and deeply provocative, reveals
itself as deceptive upon deeper reflection. Amida is
no God. He himself preaches the impersonal Absolute.[47] Opposition of persons remains penultimate,
and this is the explanation for the "convertibility of
merits";[48] once again, Samsara and Nirvana are ultimately identical.[49] "Amida" falls prey to the "temptation of all non-Christian mysticism: identity".[50]
"And yet, . . ." begins a concluding paragraph. And
yet the omnipresent grace of Christ can be effective
in an objectively inadequate way of salvation: we
recognize de Lubac's option in *Catholicisme*.

Thus is the objective analysis demanded by the
Rencontre carried out in outline fashion. The dialogue with both forms of atheism—and both are
today just as central and real—leads to an analogous
result: in both cases the interpretation of the world

[46] Am 226ff., 237ff.
[47] Am 264.
[48] Am 270f.
[49] Am 301.
[50] Am 290.

ends by destroying the human person, whether it is absorbed into the collective or is burst from within in the madness of being God (or Fate) or is dissolved in the unreality of an idealistic monism. De Lubac will provide the positive answer in large part through the works of Teilhard, whose cosmic theory of evolution is personal from its very foundations. Only the self-revealing personal God guarantees the eternal worth of the human person.

IV

THE NEWNESS OF CHRIST

"He brought all newness in bringing himself." Irenaeus' dictum about Christ, often quoted by de Lubac, may stand as the title of the attempt to understand the three great personal achievements of our author in their mutual interdependence. *Catholicisme* placed Christ's Church in a coordinate system: first, (vertical) transcendence of Christianity (as an individual historical form among others) to the totality of the world-redemption contained in it; then, (horizontal, temporal) transcendence of the time of promise to the time of fulfillment, of the Old Covenant to the New Covenant.

This motif now appears in a threefold (analogous) variation. First in the thematic of *Surnaturel*: How can man in his natural order be interiorly ordered to the fulfilling order of grace, without in the least possessing this latter in anticipation, that is, without being able to claim it for himself? Then in the thematic of the works on theological exegesis: How is the Old Covenant understanding related to the New Covenant understanding? The literal sense to the spiritual (allegorical) sense? To

what extent is the "prophecy" or typology of the
first so ordered to the second that this latter is not
contained ahead of time in the former? And finally
(taking the fundamental theological law as *analoga-
tum princeps* of the law of total cosmic evolution):
How are the macromutations of evolution, especially those from the animal realm to man, related to
the definitive mutation (at point omega) of the hu-
manized world into the divine world? Three times
the same question: first in the area of fundamental theology, then in the area of the theology of
(salvation) history, finally in the area of cosmology-
eschatology.

De Lubac testifies himself that he is thoroughly
aware that he is confronted with the same fundamental structure in the three areas of inquiry and
that he must hold his gaze directed toward the
same mystery in order to find the solution to the
question.

> "The elevation of the intelligent creature [to the
> supernatural order] surpasses a merely natural fulfill-
> ment" [Hales-Summa]. Two simple comparisons
> can help us understand this relationship. Even
> when one admits that in God's plan the entire cos-
> mic evolution has the appearance of man as its goal,
> must one necessarily conclude that this appearance
> is a *sequela creationis universi*? Or if it is true that the
> whole history of Israel is ultimately only meaning-
> ful through the coming of Jesus Christ, which it
> had prepared and to which it was wholly ordered,

is that any reason to dispute the entirely gratuitous newness of Christ's coming, even in its relationship to Israel?[1]

Here the question-complex nature/"nature-supernatural" is illuminated by that of anthropogenesis and that of the relation between Old and New Covenant. The threefold solution does not result from a mere magic formula that might be applied mechanically over and over again. Each area of inquiry must be penetratingly researched and attended to for itself in order for it to yield its proper mystery. But as each does so, the structural principle of the divine plan for the world shows itself to be a unified one.

Surnaturel

With *Surnaturel* (1946 with an *imprimatur* from 1942), a young David comes onto the field against the Goliath of the modern rationalization and reduction to logic of the Christian mystery. The sling deals a death blow, but the acolytes of the giant seize upon the champion and reduce him to silence for a long time. Not entirely without justification. The work, pieced together from many disparate preparatory studies,[2] is not completely rounded out. There are four parts. The first begins by examining the failure on the part of Baius and Jansen to

[1] MS 114.
[2] See the table in Neufeld-Sales, 64.

understand the true intention of Augustine (and his disciples, including Thomas Aquinas). In the original state, grace is "due" Adam for the perfection of his nature (Baius), or it is at least the means (in his control) for the exercise of his freedom (Jansen).[3] A juridical-naturalistic pattern of thinking is predominant here,[4] having first made its appearance in theology in the sixteenth century. In contrast to the fundamental conception of Aquinas and his age—for which the desire for the vision of God constituted the essence of the created spirit, without any "claim" being made upon God[5]—a "purely natural finality" (at least a possible one) will now be attributed to "pure spiritual nature", whereby the gratuity of grace is to be guaranteed. This occurs first with Cajetan, then Suarez and "even into our own days",[6] in an anti-Baianism that in reality remains in the undertow of Baius' formulation of the question.

This first part alone[7] will be taken up again in two later volumes, *Augustinisme et théologie moderne* and *Le Mystère du surnaturel* (1965), and made secure against all attacks.

The second part, "Spirit and Freedom in the

[3] S 23, 44.
[4] S 68.
[5] S 118.
[6] S 105ff., 148ff., 157–83.
[7] A few passages of the second part will be reworked, of course, and use made of the studies in parts 3 and 4.

Theological Tradition", will be left out—regrettably —as a kind of duplication of the first part. But it offers extremely valuable material for solidifying the thesis, beginning with the patristic-scholastic problem of freedom (both human and, especially, angelic). It is a second way of proving that Thomas, whenever he speaks of the nature of created spirit, never ascribes to it any other finality than a supernatural one. Again the concept of nature takes on a rationalistic form, at the latest in the sixteenth century, and scholastic theology is henceforth divided on the question.

The third part comprises individual studies in the prehistory and history of the concept "supernatural" (and related expressions). Though it is in evidence from the beginning with many nuances, it is first used systematically by Thomas,[8] and it is only recently that a whole treatise is built up around it[9] (from apologetic motives that do not, however, achieve their purpose).[10]

The fourth part, "Historical Remarks", adds important proof-material from the sources, most of

[8] S 327, 372, 398.

[9] "Our treatise *De Deo elevante* is not only in fact quite recent, but, with its terminology and the modes of thought this presupposes, it could not have come from an earlier period": S 422.

[10] "The more this 'supernatural order' is presented as an object of faith, the more it seems to run up against systematic rejection": S 426.

which would have belonged to the main part. And the "Conclusion" (*"Exigence divine et désir naturel"*) portrays the state of the problem for the author at that time: a couple of basic intentions that, without having to be altered, still needed clarification. It is enough here to present these intuitions, but not without first calling to mind the whole scope of the undertaking. For it is in no way concerned merely with overcoming theologically the poison of Jansenism that had smoldered for centuries in French intellectual life but rather with the poison (intended as an antidote) of a rationalism become worldwide, which treated man (and the angels) as if he were one natural being among others, of whom (following Aristotle) it was true that "the natural desire does not extend beyond what lies in the natural capacities."[11] What was devised by theologians to protect the order of grace turns, according to an inner logic, into a closed order of nature for which the "supernatural" can only be something "superadded" exteriorly[12] and thus can be dispensed with.

In contrast to this, the "Conclusion" defends the "Paradox of Man".[13] The concept of paradox, which is a central one for de Lubac, has here its most important usage by far. For the created spirit is "a unique case, for which paradox is a neces-

---

[11] Dionysius Cart.: AugThM 202; similarly Cajetan, ibid.

[12] See the study on *"Superadditum"*: S 375ff.

[13] S 483.

sary mark of truth."[14] The paradox is expressed in
the universal fundamental law of high scholasticism
that a being striving for the perfect good, even
though it requires help from another in attaining
it, is more noble than the being that can arrive at
only an imperfect good, though by its own power.[15]
In order to maintain this paradox, the idea of a
grace that is a "means to the end" *demanded* by
the "natural striving" must be overcome. This occurs through reflection: (1) on the relation between
absolute and relative being, which do not "stand
over against each other like two beings" (this is
only a "phantom of our imagination"); (2) more directly, on God's fundamental intention in creation:
to communicate himself as absolute love and to in-
scribe this wish *of his* in the innermost being of
the spiritual creature, so that it recognizes therein
the "call of God to love" and, instead of making
demands himself, stands by his very essence under
God's demand inscribed in his nature; (3) finally,
through reflection on the fact that the entire natural order stands "within" a supernatural order that
realizes this ultimate intention of God, so that every
natural demand by the creature upon God always
comes too late and is reduced to silence by the
grace already offered. (4) Everything converges in
the (Pauline-Augustinian-Ignatian) thought that we

---

[14] S 484.
[15] Summa Theol. I–II q 5, a 5, ad 2.

are not created uniquely for our own beatitude but for the glorification of the God of grace and love: "Beatitude is service, vision is adoration, freedom is dependence, possession is ecstasy." In the order of absolute love, only the law of selflessness is valid; categories such as "rights, advantages, commutative justice" are quite out of place there.[16]

The two volumes of 1965 are primarily a clearing up of numerous objections against *Surnaturel*. They separate the predominantly historical problematic (*Augustinisme et théologie moderne*) from the predominantly dogmatic problematic (*Le Mystère du surnaturel*). Three years later, de Lubac will describe the whole "nature-supernatural" terminology as "not particularly felicitous".[17] Today many prefer to speak of a "theologal order" or an "order of Covenant" or simply of the "Mystery of Christ".[18] What is essential is that in the meantime people have learned to think in more decidedly personal categories.[19] And yet the underlying question is not

---

[16] S 483–94.

[17] AthS 96.

[18] AthS 107.

[19] There is a reference to J. Mouroux, AthS 100; but de Lubac himself has used personal categories in his "*Conclusion*" (S 483). Man yearns for God as for a gift: "He desires the free and gratuitous communication of a personal being." Teilhard likewise declares himself in favor of a change of vocabulary: "The whole theory of the supernatural moves in a realm of thought that has

simply a relic of the past; the modern secularism within the Church has made it again quite relevant.

There is no need to analyze the first, historical volume, since it only expands upon the historical part of *Surnaturel* while clearing up any difficulties. It pursues the transformation of the concept of nature "microscopically, so to speak",[20] and consciously protects itself against the encyclical *Humani generis*.[21] Moreover, it is precisely here that Thomas is taken seriously as a guiding star!

In the second volume, the *"exigence"* of grace must be dealt with, and the precise scope of the *"desiderium naturale visionis"* must be determined. We can summarize only in broad strokes: (1) the creation-grace articulation, the positing of a non-divine subject that is to participate in the divine life, cannot be abandoned. For the Fathers, the articulation is the "image" (*imago*) created to become "likeness" (*similitudo*); since the Areopagite, it is the articulation between *"datum optimum"* (nature) and *"donum perfectum"* (grace), or with

---

been abandoned by most moderns. It is essential to *transpose* it into a system of representations that is understandable and vital for us." PrT 131, footnote 4. On Teilhard's corresponding categories, see PRel 170.

[20] AugThM 225.

[21] AugThM 326.

Thomas: *datio-donatio*.[22] (2) But created spiritual nature (human or angelic) cannot be understood simply as an "instance" of nature in general. One reason is that it is created immediately by God and, for this reason, immediately for God (Thomas along with the tradition);[23] another is that a spiritual nature is open to the universality of being that it both wills to know and must will to know—prior to all individual acts of free choice. In itself, the *"capacitas"* is not yet an *"appetitus perfectus"*. It is an *"aptitudo passiva"*,[24] but may not be identified with a mere *"potentia oboedientialis"*, which is proper to every nature inasmuch as it remains exposed to the free (miraculous) power of the Creator.[25] (3) This *"capacitas"* excludes, on the one hand, any inner-worldly (and thus "natural") final goal. (Thomas transforms Aristotle's final goal of inner-worldly contemplation into a purely intermediate goal.) But neither can it be satisfied by an "eternal striving" after the vision of God, an eternal asymptotic approach to this vision. (Here de Lubac parts company with Maréchal and his disciples.)[26] Such a striving would not be

[22] MS 122–23, 130.

[23] MS 146–49.

[24] MS 117.

[25] S 395ff., MS 136ff., 179ff. It is a question of the specific ontology of the "person" that first emerges as such in the light of Christianity: MS 91. On the incomparability of human nature with other natures, see already S 247, 483.

[26] MS 231ff.

"natural beatitude" but the torture of Tantalus.[27] (4) On the other hand, there is, in this *"capacitas"* that constitutes the innermost being of the created spiritual nature, no trace yet of supernatural grace or even such an orientation.[28] For this reason, de Lubac is not interested in hearing about Karl Rahner's supernatural existential. Insofar as this were to signify a "mediation" for the order of grace, "the problem would not be solved but only displaced".[29] This is in no way a denial of the fact that the concrete (*"elicited"*) act of concrete man as a movement toward his final goal is, of course, borne by grace. It is first a question only of the signature inscribed in the created spiritual nature,[30] unknown to this nature itself as created,[31] purely "habitual",[32] lying, as a "lack",[33] at the basis of all consciousness. (5) The knowledge of what the human spirit ultimately "really desires" is only communicated in the personal

[27] MS 249f.

[28] MS 55, 117.

[29] MS 136, footnote 1.

[30] Claude Bruaire gives an elucidation of this structure in his work *De l'affirmation de Dieu. Essai sur la logique de l'existence* (Seuil, 1964), which lets every human act of freedom be englobed by *"désir"*.

[31] MS 257ff. Otherwise man could conclude naturally to the order of grace from the knowledge gained through his desire; "the supernatural would be the object of natural knowledge": MS 258.

[32] MS 267.

[33] *"Per indigentiam"* (according to Thomas): MS 268.

call of the God of free grace. And with this knowledge is also communicated the possibility, itself a gift of grace, to respond to this call.[34] It is obvious that, seen biblically and theologically, this call, this free self-communication of God, is what was first intended by him: for its sake is spiritual nature created and, for the sake of this nature, the material cosmos.[35] But the whole work remains penetrated from moment to moment by God's freedom, so that the first moment (the creation of spiritual nature) does not make it "necessary" for God to pass to the second moment (grace's call).[36]

[34] MS 273ff.

[35] MS 128ff.

[36] MS 111ff. With this, de Lubac considers that he has satisfied the requirement of *Humani generis* that God could have created spiritual beings that would not have been called to a supernatural participation in God. But, he adds, such a world would have been completely different from our own (MS 105). Furthermore, even in our world grace must remain "free" with respect to nature. Therefore, the hypothesis of a "*natura pura*" (that has no "claim" to elevation) in our concrete world, where "elevation" is real and a claim *seems* to exist, is ineffectual and superfluous: MS 79–103. Nevertheless, it does not seem fully clear, after what has been said, how de Lubac can logically distinguish three moments in the Creator's plan, which as a whole is free, between which moments God's freedom would appear each time at a new level: (1) creation of spiritual being; (2) "the supernatural finality imprinted in its nature"; (3) the free offer of participation in God's life. "The first does not at all entail the second; nor does the second entail the third" (MS 112). Do not 1 and 2 coincide conceptually? And if one thinks theologically

THE NEWNESS OF CHRIST 73

At first the problematic of Thomistic *"desiderium naturale"* seemed to de Lubac to be something of an historically conditioned theologoumenon: Thomas was a "transitional author".[37] But this problematic suddenly became of great contemporary importance: once again it constitutes the fundamental concept of Teilhard de Chardin's world view. We will encounter it again there.[38]

The Senses of Scripture

De Lubac's concern with the senses of Scripture and the dialectic Old Covenant–New Covenant (eternity) dates from *Catholicisme*. The first study of the fourfold sense of Scripture was published in 1948.[39] The study that laid the foundations, treating Origen's understanding of Scripture, was published in 1950 as *Histoire et esprit*. *Exégèse médiévale I–IV* (1959/1961/1964) is its prolongation through the Middle Ages. And it finds a postlude in *Pic de la Mirandole* (1974).

---

from the starting point of the unity of God's salvific plan, is not the whole an indivisible act of God's freedom that—*in ordine executionis*—can only be conceptually analyzed into two moments—$(1 + 2) \rightarrow 3$?

[37] S 435.

[38] TMA 99; EF 94.

[39] "Sur un vieux distique. La doctrine du '*quadruple sens*' ", in: *Mélanges Cavallera* 347–66.

Let us examine the fundamental analogy to what has preceded before considering any differentiations. The relationship promise (Old Covenant)–fulfillment (New Covenant) corresponds to the relationship creation (of spiritual nature)–grace insofar as there is no *"exigence"* on the part of the Old Covenant or manifestation on the part of the New; nor is there a gradual approach to the New Covenant through progressive spiritualization (which may prevail in the Old Testament).[40] Rather is there "a discontinuity" between the two, "a rupture, the crossing of a threshold".[41]

> Israel did not become the Church little by little, naturally, as it were. The earthly Jerusalem was not changed into that Jerusalem descended from heaven, which is our mother, by a slow evolution. . . . Whatever may have been the preparation, the advances, the approaches, the decisive passage is accomplished suddenly in an act performed by Christ, a spiritual metamorphosis, without analogy in history.[42]

And this is true even though the same Holy Spirit has inspired both Testaments[43] just as the same free act of God stands behind creation and the call of grace.

[40] HE 395ff.
[41] HE 401.
[42] HE 268.
[43] HE 295ff.; ExMed III 346.

Before this new "paradox" is explained in greater detail, a word about the meaning of "Scripture" in this context is called for. Neither Origen nor any of the tradition following him understands Holy Scripture as a mere book that reports "about" past history. God's word becomes incarnate in Christ and prepares for this incarnation in Israel through the living word addressed to Abraham and to the people in the Mosaic instructions and in the prophets. This history formed by the word remains what it was, even in the time of the Church, although it now stands under the norm of a word that, in its fullness, is imbedded (in Scripture) and, as such, remains always animated by the Spirit: "*Semper enim divina Scriptura loquitur et clamat*", because it "remains always animated by the Spirit who spoke through it".[44] Scripture cannot be adequately distinguished from the Logos, even the incarnate Logos.[45] And if Origen makes a comparison between the Eucharist and Holy Scripture and seems to give Scripture priority over the Eucharist, de Lubac concurs: "For however real the [sacramental] 'body' may be, it is not the Divinity itself . . . it always remains the symbol of a more spiritual reality, while, on the other hand, the 'Word' is, in its pure essence, that reality itself. Because the Son of God, God Himself, is 'Word' ",[46] that incorporates itself both

[44] ExMed II 485 (Ps.-Ambrosius).
[45] HE 336f.
[46] HE 366.

in the spoken word of Scripture and in the Eucharist. "Finally, the Word is victorious; but this Word is beyond human words and rites: it is the speaking Word."[47] For this reason the theory of the senses of Scripture is not a curiosity of the history of theology but an instrument for seeking out the most profound articulations of salvation history. When Scripture is so conceived, the notion that it is sufficient for the complete interpretation of revelation, and thereby also for the construction of the whole of theology, can hold true from antiquity through the Middle Ages to the Reformation.[48] In this it was, of course, self-evident that Scripture is read by the Church and by the individual only within the Church: "*figurata sacramenta* [*Scripturae*] *non alibi aperiuntur nisi intra Ecclesiam*",[49] who applies, in this process, her own norm (*regula fidei*).[50] This means for her in practice that individual passages can only be interpreted from the vision of the whole, from the insight into the catholic context.[51] Her "Spirit" is after all the one and only Spirit, Christ's, who expresses and interprets himself in the sign.[52]

[47] HE 372.
[48] ExMed I 56ff.
[49] Autpertus: ExMed I 58.
[50] ExMed IV 90ff.
[51] ExMed IV 93.
[52] HE 277; ExMed II 650; see III 196: "Christianity is not properly speaking a 'book religion'; it is the religion of the Word

For Origen[53] and the entire Middle Ages following him,[54] the guarantee for the fundamental
distinction—between literal and spiritual (or allegorical) sense—is Paul. Hence, however strongly
pagan extrabiblical[55] or Jewish (philosophical)[56] influences may have played a part for Origen and
again in the Middle Ages,[57] the elements that originate here remain secondary. They are clearly subor-
dinated to the biblical understanding and substan-
tially Christianized. Two triple schemata compete
with each other in Origen: (1) historical-moral-

---

but not uniquely, not even primarily, of the Word in its written
form; it is the religion of the Logos, 'not written and mute, but
the incarnate and living Logos'. (Bernard)." Another theme
should be mentioned here, powerfully introduced by Origen
and continued in the Middle Ages (ExMed III 346): according
to this, the prophets and saints of the Old Covenant would have
shared, in looking forward to it, the Spirit of Christ; they would
have seen by anticipation his mysteries but would have hidden
them under a veil by reason of the "economy". This thought
is more reported than taken up systematically by de Lubac.
Otherwise the principle of Christ's total newness, which he
brings with himself (beginning with his Incarnation!) would
be brought into question—and the analogy to the principle of
Surnaturel and to the apology of Teilhard would thereby also
collapse.
   [53] HE 69ff.
   [54] ExMed II 668f., 675f.
   [55] HE 159f.
   [56] HE 162.
   [57] ExMed IV 182 and passim.

mystical sense; and (2) historical-mystical-moral
sense. The first schema follows the anthropologi-
cal trichotomy (preferred by Philo) of body-soul-
spirit and reflects a pattern of ascent that progresses
through the purifications of the soul (morality) to
spiritual-mystical knowledge. But this schema,
which persists—unsystematically—into the Middle
Ages,[58] remains, in Christian theology, in the service of the second: history (the letter = OT)-allegory
(the mystery of Christ = NT)-the life of the Church;
to which is joined, as fourth sense, anagogy: by
which the entire earthly salvation history is related
vertically to eternity, the consummated kingdom of
God. But in Christian theology, the third and fourth
moments only form the unfolding of the inner fullness of the mystery of Christ, so that ultimately
what remains is again only the two Pauline moments, letter and spirit, type and truth. And truth
here is both "ahead"[59] (within history)—insofar as
the Old Testament hastens toward the New and the
New toward its definitive and manifest fulfillment
at the "end of time"—and "above", insofar as eternal life has begun with the New Testament's end-
time.[60] In the Middle Ages (under the influence
of the Areopagite) the upward orientation to the
"above" (mysticism of ascent) often holds a danger-
ous predominance over the historical-eschatologi-

[58] ExMed I 139ff.
[59] HE 291.
[60] See the Barth quotation: ExMed I 309.

cal dimension.[61] At the end of *Histoire et esprit*, the further "history and decay" of the theorem of the fourfold sense of Scripture is recounted in a brief summary.[62] As the author then began to work through the immense material, it proved to be richer and more varied than was at first supposed. For when exegesis is understood in this way, it includes all of theology, from its historical foundation to its most spiritual summits.[63] In the center stands Christ, who is both exegete and exegesis; he interprets himself and does so primarily in deeds, which are incarnate words.[64] Thus the letter is always being transformed into spirit, promise into fulfillment, in a unique transition, by a mutation that is at the same time conversion[65] and also the condensation of the manifold in the uniquely normative center.[66] The second volume develops broadly the problematic of each of the four dimensions of the senses of Scripture. (Particularly worthy of note is the connection between "*historia*" and "*kenosis*",[67] the indispensability of history,[68] the understanding of allegory as the meaning coinciding

[61] ExMed II 621ff.
[62] HE 410–29.
[63] ExMed II 478.
[64] ExMed I 322f.
[65] ExMed I 311.
[66] ExMed I 327, III 181: the doctrine of the "*Verbum abbreviatum*".
[67] ExMed II 454.
[68] ExMed II 470.

with faith,[69] the persistence of the two functions of the tropological sense: morality as means of ascent and as unfolding of the mysterial sense,[70] and the already-mentioned double dimension of the anagogical sense.[71] But all these dimensions of the sense of Scripture are inseparable from each other; they interpenetrate each other.)[72]

The third part investigates both the supposed and the real development of the theory. Modern exegetes (Spicq, for example) would have been happy to ascertain a gradual development of "exact science" in the Middle Ages. De Lubac shows the error of such a notion in three initial chapters but recognizes with the beginning of the tendency toward the "*summa*" (in Hugh of St. Victor) a crisis in the way exegesis-theology had been conceived up until that time. There is an "*éclatement*":[73] the "*littera*" has the tendency to become the independent science of exegesis; the "*allegoria*" tends to become dogmatic theology; the "*tropologia-anagogia*" tends to become spirituality and mystical theology (especially when Dionysius is definitively victorious over Augustine in the late Middle Ages).[74] The final chapter is devoted to Joachim, with whom the great change will

[69] ExMed II 489.
[70] ExMed II 549.
[71] ExMed II 621ff.
[72] ExMed II 648.
[73] ExMed III 418.
[74] ExMed III 421, 429ff.

come about, at first unnoticed but soon recogniz-
able in what follows. A change that will threaten
the Church as institution, give birth to spiritual
churches and enlightenments, and finally produce
atheistic messianism.

The fourth volume reaches its high point in
its presentation of Bonaventure and then Thomas,
who summarizes luminously but brings "nothing
new",[75] and in the revival of a spiritual interpretation
of Scripture with the humanists, especially Erasmus.[76] In between lies the gradual but inexorable
loss of inner vitality and the mechanical sclerosis of
the theory of the four senses,[77] its complete "decadence",[78] the unjustified fame of a Nicholas of Lyra
and his imitators.[79] The outcome of de Lubac's
portrayal of history is not at all the wish for a slav-
ish renewal of the old schema—the outward form
theology has taken is no longer capable of being
forced into such a mold. The result has been rather
a rethinking of the synthesis that lived within the
schema, of the breadth of the spiritual horizon, the
enduring value of the main articulations; the theology of the present and of the future will have to
emulate all this.[80]

[75] ExMed IV 285ff.
[76] ExMed IV 427ff.
[77] ExMed IV 310–17.
[78] ExMed IV 369ff.
[79] ExMed IV 344ff.
[80] It must be at least noted that the ancient and humanistic

One can describe the numerous works de Lubac devoted to the person and work of his friend Teilhard de Chardin as being written to meet particular circumstances. The most important are *La Pensée religieuse du Père Teilhard de Chardin* (1962), *La Prière du Père Teilhard de Chardin* (1964, with a "*Note sur l'apologétique teilhardienne*"), *Blondel et Teilhard de Chardin* (1965, with the articles included there), *Teilhard, Missionnaire et apologiste* (1966), *L'Eternel féminin* (1968, including "*Teilhard et notre temps*").[81] They were meant to obviate numerous misunderstandings and the danger of being placed on the Index. But in reality they are more than that. With

---

substructure of early Christian thought and early and high medieval thought is always taken into consideration. With Origen it is the confrontation with Philo; in the early Middle Ages the encouragement of ancient poetry (I 66f.), the allegory of the "beautiful prisoner" (Dt 21:10–14), which, like the "*spolia Aegyptorum*", is applied to the Christian use of pagan literary treasures (I 290f.), the sense for profane and sacred symbolism (IV 125ff.), the appreciation of extrabiblical prophecies (the Sybyls, and so on), the particular esteem of Vergil ("*Vergile philosophe et prophète*", IV 233–62). Without attending to these and other concurrent themes, one would fail to understand the breadth of de Lubac's spirit.

[81] In addition: the editions, with commentary, of *Lettres d'Egypte* (1963), *Ecrits du temps de la guerre (1916–1919)* (1965), *Lettres intimes* (1974), and numerous articles: *Bibliographie* 188, 306, 204, 206, 199a, 308, 239, 253.

all the reservations made throughout with respect to frequent inconsistencies in the progression of thought or in expression,[82] Teilhard's work nevertheless provides an occasion to develop more intensively a whole dimension—the cosmic dimension of Catholicism—in de Lubac's thought.

Teilhard is a visionary; he is a scientist; but not least is he a great and conscious apologist who was concerned, as was de Lubac, to reflect upon creation on as noble a scale as possible—and thus upon the Creator. His ambition was to propose a "mysticism of the West" as an alternative to the apersonal-atheistic mysticism of the East and to modern Western atheism.[83] A mysticism that would

---

[82] PRel expresses it thus: "We cannot flatter ourselves as being able to be counted among Father Teilhard's disciples." De Lubac announces his misgivings in a great number of places. A whole chapter treats Teilhard's "limits" (PrT 109ff.). The concept of creation remains unclear: PRel 288; it is the same with original sin: PRel 167; the "*durcissement*" of the last years is often spoken of (PRel 117, 142f., 174, 264); also simplifications (PRel 216, 269), omissions (PRel 270f.), ambiguity (PrT 101; PRel 79, 80; EF 168), an urge to systematize that nevertheless does not result in a "fixed, closed system" (PRel 20), a dangerously biological vocabulary (PRel 273ff., 305), an exaggerated accentuation of the collective (AthS 141, EF 86f.), playing with the thought of the Superman (PRel 303), racial mutation within the historical period (PRel 301). The processes foreseen for the future of the noosphere do not seem evident to de Lubac (PRel 307); there is much that sounds "almost like mythology" (PRel 310). In PrT such restrictive remarks are met throughout.

[83] TMA 151. He can outline a work in three parts: physics,

be personal down to its very roots. The incarnation of God in Jesus Christ occupies the central position in the world. Both the inner-historical and the eschatological nature of this position let the entire world genesis converge upon Christ, in an ascending movement from matter to life to personal spirit. In the genesis of spirit the movement is at the same time realization (of what was potential). "Christ is more real than every other reality of this world", says Teilhard,[84] echoing the sentiments of the author of *Histoire et esprit* and *Corpus mysticum* for whom the "spiritual" is more real than the "material", which is only type, symbol, Old Testament of the intelligible or spiritual. And so for Teilhard, who is close to Leibniz here, matter is the unconscious "germ" of the spirit, and the qualitative leaps in evolution, when a leap has become possible and its time has arrived through preparatory maturations, are ones of "concentration", of "reflection", of a coming to consciousness. The decisive step of personalization does not, however, signify the disintegration of life into individual centers, for God's plan of creation completes the edifice that has been begun by Christ, who is the keystone and who integrates into his

---

apologetics, mysticism: PrT 147; see the chapter "*Personalisme*" in PRel 201–14. The idea of personalism solidifies only gradually: ibid., 208.

[84] PRel 91, see 290.

mystical or eucharistic body all persons (who let themselves be inserted in his universal person).[85] The world is "thus held together ultimately only from above".[86] Evolution, as coherent, only becomes possible through what comes last, the omega of evolution. It is the final synthesis that explains everything, and Teilhard attempts to build up his "proof of God" by starting here.[87] In this he joins Blondel on a central issue. Blondel has expressed the same thought while writing about Leibniz' *Vinculum substantiale*:[88] the entire universe attains its real, substantial footing ultimately only in the person of the God-man. De Lubac has gathered Blondel's numerous references to his "panchristism" in the note to a letter to Valensin.[89] The exchange of letters between Blondel and Teilhard (through Valensin), which de Lubac has provided with a very careful commentary, presupposes this common basis. They are concerned above all with the "how" of the world's transition to its definitive transfigured state. To Blondel, Teilhard seems to accentuate the

[85] Teilhard did not teach an apocatastasis and did not shrink from the thought of a "definitive loss", a possible damnation: PRel 162, 166; PrT 71.

[86] PRel 13.

[87] TMA 69.

[88] As a thesis in Latin, 1893; taken up in "*Une Enigme historique: le 'Vinculum substantiale' d'après Leibniz et l'ébauche d'un réalisme supérieur*" (1930).

[89] B-V I 43–48; more in H. Bouillard, *Blondel et le Christianisme* (1961), 200ff.

continuity too much and the break in continuity too little. But when Teilhard speaks of point omega, it is necessary to distinguish precisely an immanent and a transcendent omega; the former is the maturation of the universe toward a critical end-point; the latter is the transition that can only be explained transcendentally (from above): Christ's parousia.[90] Continuity—but "completely recast".[91] And so Teilhard can propose to Blondel, as the eloquent image of his own world view:

> All the world's effort can be interpreted as the preparation for a sacrifice. . . . The only Millenarianism I can foresee is that of an era when men have become conscious of their unity in *all* men and their intimate connection with all else and can thus freely throw the fullness of their souls into the divine conflagration. All our work strives ultimately to prepare the sacrificial host upon which the divine fire must descend.[92]

And elsewhere: "The world can only reach you, Lord, by a type of inversion, a turning back, an excentration in which for a time not only the success of individuals but even the appearance of any human advantage founders. . . ."[93]

The notion of the positivity and fruitfulness of the "passivities" can be added here. It is expressed

[90] PRel 249ff., 259ff.; AthS 136–37.
[91] EF 134.
[92] B-T 43.
[93] PRel 182.

particularly in *Le Milieu divin* but elsewhere as well and has been brought into sharp focus by de Lubac. It is not only unavoidable suffering that is fruitful (even more so than active achievements),[94] not only death consciously offered, but also contemplation as such is active in the deepest interior of the world;[95] and parallel to a more profound fidelity to the earth is an even more profound "detachment".[96] If the drive "forward" is also a type of "obsession" for Teilhard,[97] it is nevertheless always simultaneously a drive "upward and forward",[98] and this stands in the fundamental eschatological tension of Catholicism (the "already" of Christ's existence in the transfiguration and the Eucharist and the "not yet" of the consummation of his mystical body). The material world, in its state of becoming, must "disappear" for Teilhard's eschatological impatience; it is enough for this that "the Spirit change zones, and the figure of the world will immediately be altered."[99] Teilhard's world vision comes close here to an idealism of Buddhist stamp, but the christological, personal, and historical realism prevents this collapse.

[94] PrT 75–79; PRel 43f., 123, 326.
[95] PRel 318ff.
[96] PRel 135–37.
[97] PRel 141–42.
[98] PRel 140, 236, 292.
[99] PRel 191.

De Lubac's whole problematic of the "*desiderium naturale*" appears in a radical form with Teilhard: the entire universe from its lowest level as pure matter is nothing else but this.[100] In his detailed commentary on Teilhard's hymn to the "Eternal Feminine", which celebrates the ascent of the feminine principle from the *matrix-materia* through the naturally fruitful woman (and all the preliminary stages of sexuality) to the fruitfulness of the Virgin Mary through God, de Lubac finds again his own problematic: nature as essentially a longing and transcendence by virtue of the ordination to a transcendent, uniquely fulfilling principle. He is concerned in all his writings on Teilhard with Teilhard's fundamental "catholic" vision. In the question of whether Teilhard had any metaphysical position at all, or a genuine but hidden one, and what his method actually was, de Lubac is prepared to make any reasonable concession.[101] But not on anything that involves his orthodoxy. Teilhard was a decided anti-modernist.[102] Only by holding fast to the dogma of Chalcedon—Christ's divine humanity in its qualitative difference from the grace given to all other men—do Christians have the op-

[100] TMA 101f; PRel 257; EF 117: all three passages draw the parallels to the "*desiderium naturale*" in Thomas.

[101] PRel 96, 116ff., 231ff., 257; on the method, PRel 229–47; PrT 109–21; on Teilhard's own awareness of the limitations, B-T 118–26.

[102] PrT 197.

portunity, but also the responsibility, of recognizing and showing humanity the way out of the dead-
ends of evolution.[103]

[103] PrT 118, 179; PRel 55f.

V

CREATURE AND PARADOX

While de Lubac, in the three areas of research we have described, made himself the defender of misunderstood and unappreciated themes and currents in the history of theology and presented his own thought only indirectly, this thought comes forth unconcealed in several shorter works of the middle period. In 1945, a small collection of *Paradoxes* was published, to which was added, in 1954, a second collection, *Nouveaux paradoxes*. Also in 1945 (with an *imprimatur* from 1941), *De la connaissance de Dieu* was published; augmented in 1948 after arousing senseless enmity, it was published in its final form in 1956 under the title *Sur les chemins de Dieu*. This form, with its many protective measures, made it somewhat less apt for its original purpose, which was to be a small handbook for modern intellectuals seeking God, since it had to be burdened with an abundance of patristic-scholastic annotations. The *Paradoxes* remained essentially undisturbed.[1]

[1] Expanded edition in one volume, 1959. The *Chemins de Dieu* are justified against the senseless attacks in an "epilogue" in which modesty and self-confidence are beautifully combined.

We experience in these works more of the original point of departure for the author's thought,
although it was already sketched out, especially in
Catholicisme and *Surnaturel*. This point of departure
is certainly "Augustinian", when one views Augustine as the "pinnacle of the patristic age"[2] and
the most important inspiration of the Middle Ages
and even the modern period.[3] But de Lubac—and
this is part of his "Augustinianism"—is profoundly
aware of the mortality of all historical systems of
thought. The great minds leave their inscription
upon the history of thought, but "as soon as their
work is 'surpassed' it is also already misunderstood.
Although we have their texts in our hands, we
lack the imagination to reconstruct their mental
universe. To do that we would have to rely on that
which, in our very depths, has been newly recast."
With Augustine, we are hardly able to understand
in our turn what he meant by "*intelligentia fidei*"—
"the soul and moving force of all Augustinianism".
This mean between the supernatural "mystical il-
lumination" of a holy soul and "rational elaboration by theologians or philosophers" no longer
seems to be within our grasp.[4] But the relationship of these two poles engages de Lubac's interest
constantly: the dynamism of the "restless heart"

---

[2] CMy 262.
[3] Przywara: *Augustinisch*, 2d ed. (1970).
[4] CMy 263.

ineradicably present deep within,[5] of that "habitual" longing for the absolute[6] that "breathes" in
the soul,[7] preceding every act of thinking and willing,[8] without, however, being an ("ontological")
vision of absolute being,[9] but ever under the necessity of expressing itself in rational notions and concepts, conclusions, modes of proof, and systems,
in order to make its antecedently given content
clear to itself reflexively, although it can never ex-
haust or embrace this content in these unavoidable forms. One sees the proximity to Blondel and
Maréchal: "There is always more in the concept
than the concept itself."[10] "We have a power of
affirmation that surpasses both our power to con-
ceive and our power to argue."[11] "Prior to all dialectic . . . our spirit already affirms God."[12] With
Thomas: "In every act of thought and will, God is
also thought and willed implicitly." Two dimensions are always present in this primordial core
and source of created nature: an incomprehensi-
ble "presence",[13] despite all "improbability",[14] "im-

[5] Ch 213f.
[6] Ch 16.
[7] Ch 51.
[8] Ch 13f.
[9] Ch 249.
[10] Ch 111; for Maréchal and Blondel: 91.
[11] Ch 133.
[12] Ch 134.
[13] Ch 46–48.
[14] Ch 59.

perturbable";[15] a continuous "revelation",[16] that persists in the subject and throughout every object;[17] a "having-been-grasped"[18] of which one ultimately cannot say whether it is the Spirit that urges him from within to the eternal movement of emergence or attracts him from without.[19] And this—as in *Surnaturel*—is a description of the primordial phenomenon even "before" all "elevation" by grace.

That is the presupposition. And now what is properly the thesis of the book, in which its pathos becomes evident: the primordial knowledge (the certitude of primordial "faith")[20] can only come to itself in reflexive concepts that, as indeed valid but never sufficient, must always be criticized, relativized, submitted to the principle of analogy. Here the right and necessity of negative theology is established! And yet to carry through this criticism, the orientation to the primordial certitude, ever beyond the concept, is always necessary. And so the fundamental thesis is twofold: (1) the strict rejection of all reduction of God's living conscious-

[15] Ch 44f.
[16] Ch 15.
[17] Ch 109.
[18] Ch 158.
[19] Ch 257, the final sentence.
[20] Ch 44f. At times he can speak of "*intuitivité primordiale et simple*" (Ch 102) or of "*un fond d'intuition*" (Ch 249) (both are quotations), but he immediately adds that there is "*aucune 'vision intellectuelle' directe de l'Être, aucune intuition qui se suffise*" (Ch 249) for the natural man here below.

ness to logical categories—Hegel's "absolute knowledge" is a self-contradiction for de Lubac[21]—and
thus all the more a rejection of every superficial,
self-satisfied philosophical or theological positivism;
(2) the assignment of all negative theology to its
proper place—the *via negationis* can only be en-
tered upon because an *"eminentia"* is already present
within the *"positio"* to call forth the necessary criticism.[22] Each side of the thesis requires the other.
Proofs for God are necessary, as reflexive thought
and deduction are necessary. Genuine steps are
taken (beyond mere "analysis" of what is already
known),[23] although in this process what was always already present is only brought into the light;
the concept of God cannot be "generated" out of
something else.[24] Not even through "dialectics",[25]
which de Lubac of course recognizes as a method of
thought but rejects as a way to God: the conceptual
beings posited by dialectical thought have "no interior" and are only "terms that are relative to all the
others with which they stand in the series",[26] un-
less one recognizes behind the conceptual dialectic

[21] Ch 86ff., 248.
[22] Ch 248–49.
[23] Ch 72.
[24] Ch 19ff., 251. Thus the pointed rejection of all psycholog-
ical, psychoanalytical, sociological (and so forth) derivations of
the God concept.
[25] Ch 41.
[26] Ch 42.

the *"inquiétude"* of the soul toward God that drives the whole process forward. The "valid!" proofs for God have inner limits;[27] as part of a system they are "mortal"[28] and must be rethought in ever new efforts in order to remain alive.[29] The atheistic denial is a stimulus for this,[30] particularly in its Marxist form.[31] But this effort makes it clear that in true Christian thought, the "mystical" and the "intellectual" moments are never separable. They arise from each other (as is emphatically shown with respect to Aquinas) in a tension but only to manifest anew how much more profoundly they belong together.[32] The same unity in tension is pointed out for poetry and philosophy, mysticism and theology,[33] philosophical and spiritual considerations of God.[34] The position taken against the "two atheisms" finds its ultimate justification here: no Buddhist evasion in purely individual intuition and no Marxist alienation of the person in a collective constructed purely by reason.[35] A world without transcendence is unlivable. The critique of a self-absolutizing negative theology that is then

[27] Ch 99–100.
[28] Ch 202ff.
[29] Ch 104; on the ontological argument: Ch 95–98.
[30] Ch 220.
[31] Ch 208–10.
[32] Ch 167–75.
[33] Ch 115.
[34] Ch 135, 152–53.
[35] Ch 226.

tempted to flirt with these atheisms stands as a
warning against anticipating prematurely the negative moment in the path of God.[36] The purification
of concepts is indeed necessary[37] but always presupposes the original assent.[38]

Finally, and decisively: the original and necessary impulse toward transcendence presupposes
the mystery-presence of an absolute being that can
only be adored.[39] No mere conceptual edifice, however religious it may be, will ever take the place
of this adoration. The primordial phenomenon
can only be interpreted personally: Being is the
Other.[40] All law points toward something good,
and what is good points toward the one who is
good.[41] He must reveal himself for man to have
a participation in him; only the God of the Bible
—over against all the gods of philosophy and religion—is the living God.[42] The saint gives a witness
to him that surpasses in structure and force every
rational proof. It touches me in my most inward
"*desiderium naturale Dei*".[43] It raises the innermost
need of adoration into the light.

This leads us directly into the fundamental

[36] Ch 143.
[37] Ch 128–29.
[38] Ch 130f., 145, 149, 151f., 157, 48.
[39] Ch 176.
[40] Ch 117–18.
[41] Ch 120–22.
[42] Ch 221, 206.
[43] Ch 180, 181, 182f., 185f., 187, 211.

meaning of the paradox that, as a thought-form, is developed and put through its paces in many secular and above all Christian examples in the two volumes whose titles derive from this paradox. Opposing expressions bring to light in the conceptual realm the ever-greater richness of the original phenomenon. Without actually contradicting one another, both sets of expressions are justified—but neither do they "fuse into each other" dialectically.[44] Instead, together, they point beyond themselves to the phenomenon that lies both "beneath" and "above" them. There is a clear kinship with Guardini's *Gegensatz* [opposition], but with Guardini, the form is predominant; with de Lubac, the Augustinian dynamic. The paradox "does not sin against logic, whose laws remain intact; but the paradox escapes its domination".[45] It is the "enduring flavor of paradox" that maintains "the truth in the state of its original freshness".[46] Let us take an example of the use of paradox: the relationship of the sacred to the profane in the Christian era.

> Two things are demanded of us: that we "rediscover the sense of the sacred" and that we "integrate the sacred into all our daily life". These are certainly two opposed aspirations—although, of course, all reality can (and should) be sacralized, the universe has as a whole a sacred goal, and the Resurrection

[44] NP 71f., 73f.
[45] NP 143.
[46] NP 153.

of Jesus has become the promise of its resurrection. But not everything is, so to speak, sacred by nature. If the holy were everywhere, it would soon no longer be anywhere. Or it becomes a very ambiguous "sacred" that one ought rather to flee than to "rediscover".[47]

We find the explanation of the paradoxical demand upon Christians in two steps: in the background, the misunderstanding of a homogeneous sacrality of nature (which, however, is now elevated to the supernatural); before us, at the same time, the demand to turn our gaze toward the eschatological; and set in relief against this, the particularity of the Church—contemporaneity of "already" and "not yet". The relation between text and interpretation reminds one of the *Chemins*: the text is "prospective, virtually infinite"; interpretation is reflexive; it goes "farther than the text in analyzing it into its elements" and yet can never go beyond the text whose "concrete richness always outweighs the commentary" and therefore calls for ever-further interpretation.[48] The *Chemins* are also brought to mind by the reflection on being and concept,[49] existence and reason,[50] Christianity's historical continuity and its newness,[51] rationalism as domesti-

[47] NP 162f.
[48] NP 82.
[49] NP 102f.
[50] NP 99; see NP 128 on love and technology.
[51] NP 169ff.

cation of the spirit,[52] Marxism[53] and Buddhism,[54] and the relation between Church and state (the Church is neither for nor against power).[55] More central are the sharp rejections of modern slogans and programs for a "socially committed", "totally incarnated" Christianity.[56] It is easy to show that here only one side of the Christian paradox is seen and then made absolute.

The *"Paradoxes"*, however, have yet another side. They let us into the author's soul; indirectly, perhaps, yet more deeply than other works. They give us a glimpse of his fundamental decision in both personal and intellectual matters. The chapter on suffering betrays a great deal of the inner sufferings of one unjustly persecuted, wrongly accused.[57] The call to spiritual boldness,[58] and at the same time to "modesty"[59] and even "inconspicuousness",[60] characterizes his personal paradox. The intention of his

[52] NP 179.

[53] P 46f., NP 109.

[54] P 60.

[55] P 61.

[56] P 41ff., 57ff. Against Christians who "understand" atheism: 174f.

[57] NP 135ff.

[58] NP 75–76, 165.

[59] NP 84.

[60] P 28: "Authentic personality is only acquired by virtue of willed impersonality and abnegation in research; and extended influence—in this sense impersonal—is only obtained thanks to this personality." See chapter on "Disinterestedness", P 49ff.

book is visible in the following expression: "Potential mystics, or mystics in a primitive state, are scattered in the world. These, above all, are the ones who must be reached. And, by definition, they do not belong to any 'public'."[61] For the last thing that de Lubac wanted to be was a publicity seeker.[62] "Nothing is more opposed to witness than vulgarization. Nothing is more unlike the apostolate than propaganda."[63] We experience what a true theology is for de Lubac,[64] what specific gravity the Church's tradition has for him. ("In order to escape the outworn ideas that pass themselves off as tradition, one must go back into the farthest past—which will reveal itself to be the nearest present."[65] But "the intellectual effort of our Fathers does not dispense us from an analogous effort."[66] "Archeology", with its laborious and dusty excavations, cannot simply be dispensed with; rather it is necessary in order to reach the wellsprings of living water.[67] Yet, even in all the effort of seeking the living origins, the paradox of the ever-greater always remains: "The great effort consists in striving to discover Christianity in its fullness and in its purity. . . .

[61] P 22.
[62] P 21.
[63] P 19.
[64] P 23f.
[65] P 11.
[66] P 33.
[67] P 38.

Like God himself, it is always there, present in its entirety, but it is we who are always more or less absent. It escapes us to the extent that we think we possess it."[68]

This keen awareness of both truths—that the living mystery expresses itself in historical forms and that the mystery always transcends these forms —gives de Lubac his inimitable superiority without loss of the larger overview, of prudence, or of sober judgment. He can become enthusiastic, but he never becomes the captive of his hero or idea. He goes into the most minute details without ever losing the sense of catholicity. With everyone he is as polite as he is fearless. He is, in the French sense of the word, a mystic who nevertheless has always before his eyes the dangers and temptations of all non-Catholic mysticism.[69]

In this he recognizes his close bonds with the friend to whom he erected a memorial in his *Images de l'abbé Monchanin* (1966). This priest-poet—out of whose writings a book entitled *From Asceticism to Mysticism* has been put together—heard in his heart the call to dedicate himself to a life of contemplation in the spiritual realm of India. He did this with unconditional dedication but with a precise discernment of spirits: "The Church's first duty is adoration, an act that is only an anticipation, a foretaste,

[68] P 37.
[69] Am 290f., 295.

and a 'repetition' of the eternal life in the bosom of the Most Holy Trinity."[70] Adoration, not a seeking after identity. Union, but within the mystery of the eternal distinction of the Divine Persons. He named his Indian hermitage after them—*Saccitananda*: *sat* is origin; *cit* is Logos; *ananda* is beatitude (as a symbol for the Spirit). He lived the seven years in India interiorly in a "long and bitter purification",[71] in the will to take nights upon himself, in substitution, for the spiritual aberrations of his chosen homeland. And although he sought union with God, he was nonetheless very reserved in regard to the use of yoga methods within Christian contemplation.[72] Only by passing through a purifying, transforming fire—this is also de Lubac's constant admonition—can the fruit of non-Christian thought become usable for the Church and Christ.

[70] IM 75.
[71] IM 97.
[72] IM 94–95; see Jules Monchanin, *Mystique de l'Inde, Mystère chrétien* (1974), 257f.

VI

THE CHURCH

The Church stands clearly in the center of what we can call de Lubac's late work. She was always present before, but somewhat in the way she was present to the Fathers of the Church: as what was always presupposed, implicitly present in every thought, never thematically reflected upon at length. In spite of this, we must acknowledge in looking back upon the whole work that she is the real center of his whole life's work: the meeting point of God's descending world and man's world ascending to him. The thematic treatment of the Church was occasioned by an historical event: the Council, at which de Lubac—his theological authority fully reestablished—was an active collaborator; and the postconciliar confusion in the Church, stemming from the Council; distortions, oversimplifications and misinterpretations that must have dismayed the great universalist that de Lubac is and brought him to apply the fundamental theological insights he had gained earlier to this present situation of the Church. It is unnecessary to say that this late work, which understandably broaches no fundamentally new themes, is written with the same painstaking care, supported by the same overflowing abundance of texts from all epochs of the Church, as all that de Lubac had worked upon earlier. If the work of the middle years was that of a man suffering from persecution by men representing the Church, the later works are those of one who is suffering from the state of the Church as a whole. If Bernanos has the pastor of Torcy say to his young colleague that his place within the mystery of Jesus is the Garden of Olives, then it would not be going far astray to say that de Lubac's place is the court of the *praetorium*, the pillar of scourging. The spirit in which he bore the blows—in contrast to many contemporaries—can be shown by a passage in the book that forms the prelude to the series of works yet to be considered: *Méditation sur l'Eglise* (1953).

> It is possible that many things, in the human aspect of the Church, disappoint us. It can also happen that we can be profoundly misunderstood without being at fault ourselves. It is possible that, even within her, we have to suffer persecution. . . . Patience and loving silence will be of more value than all else; we need not fear the judgment of those who do not see the heart, and we will think that the Church never gives us Jesus Christ in a better way than in the opportunities she offers us to be conformed to his Passion. . . . The trial will perhaps be heavier if it comes, not from the

malice of a few men, but from a situation that might appear inextricable: for then neither a generous forgiveness nor the forgetting of one's own person is sufficient to overcome it. Let us nevertheless be happy, before "the Father who sees in secret", to participate in this way in that *Veritatis unitas* that we implore for all on Good Friday.[1]

The Splendor of the Church provides, as it were, the spirituality for the theology of *Catholicisme*. The mystery of the Church is set in relief against the entire mystery of salvation as its existential center. Her particular mystery is first reflected upon, and consequences are then drawn for Christian life in two particularly penetrating chapters (7 and 8), before the final chapter takes up a theme that will be heard repeatedly from now on: the Church and Mary. The entire work is preconciliar but seems to move toward the theology of the Council in great strides, plotting out by anticipation sure guidelines for its groping. The Church as "a mystery"[2] (chapter 1): the distinction between *foi* and *croyance*, and the theme "*credere in . . .*" appear already here; both will be further developed at a later date.[3] Everything in the Church is "contrast and

[1] M 164.

[2] M 9–37. *Paradoxe et mystère de l'Eglise* will elaborate more precisely the fact that the Church is a (secondary) aspect of the one mystery of Jesus Christ: PME 30–58.

[3] M 20–25; see FCh, chapter 4, 149ff.

paradox";[4] the dimensions of her mystery (chapter 2) prevent any oversimplifying definition. She has an "eternal" side but also a perishable one that ought not to be eternalized.[5] Above all (chapter 3) the Church as *ecclesia* is both *convocatio* (from above, from God) and *congregatio* (of men, from below);[6] she is invisible-visible, formed by a hierarchical structure established from above ("people" of God is therefore a possible description but not the central one for the Church);[7] her theology will always remain antidonatist.[8] There lies at the heart of the Church an ineradicable complementarity: the Church (through her hierarchical office) "makes the Eucharist", and the "Eucharist makes the Church" as incorporation into Christ's body.[9] For this reason, the Eucharist can only be genuine in the Church.[10] From here, the two sides of the Church's polarity will be developed once again: the Church in the midst of the world (chapter 5) is irreducible to the state, just as man has an irreducibly twofold orientation: to God and to the world.[11] The Church's orientation to God frees man ever anew

[4] M 36.
[5] M 50ff.
[6] M 78.
[7] M 81.
[8] M 86.
[9] M 103.
[10] M 122. Here as little as elsewhere does de Lubac go more closely into ecumenical problems arising in this respect.
[11] M 129.

from every quasi-divine absolutizing of state and
culture; and she does it in a preeminent way through
her hierarchy: the papacy guarantees the freedom
of the bishops with respect to civil leaders.[12] The
Church is the herald of unity in the face of all na-
tionalism, a unity that is never merely inner-worldly
but also never merely supra-worldly. Social work
and adoration go hand in hand.[13] Since the demar-
cation between ecclesial and secular competences
can never be established with mathematical exac-
titude, the Church in the world always remains a
militant Church, even if she restricts herself more
resolutely than before to the spiritual (as her formal
object). But the Church remains the "sacrament
of Christ" (chapter 6): leading to him and at the
same time effectively containing him. And therefore
she is, for each individual, not only a pedagogue
leading to Christ: she "remains always present to
the dialogue of the soul with its Lord".[14] She will
never—as Joachim held—be surpassed in her visible
form. Theology will never be reducible to anthropology[15] nor the mystery of the Church to sociol-
ogy.[16]

There follow now the two existential chapters.
First the truly magnificent—at the end, hymnlike—

[12] M 134.
[13] M 140ff.
[14] M 158.
[15] M 173.
[16] M 174.

portrayal of the *homo ecclesiasticus*, in which a wisdom is unfolded that anticipates and responds to all postconciliar objections and criticisms; the reactionary or hypercritical attitude, arrogance, ambition, the temptation to mere social work, or, at the other extreme, to a merely charismatic elite. The Church is a narrow gate: like Augustine and Newman, one must bend down to enter her. Finally (chapter 9), the intimate connection between the Church (as virgin, bride of God, mother) and Mary: as it is found in the great tradition; the interpretation of the *Song of Songs* as applying to the Church, Mary, the believing soul.[17]

Almost all the themes of the late works have already been touched upon here, so that we can now summarize more briefly. The alarm over the chaos breaking out within the Church, as expressed in *L'Eglise dans la crise actuelle* (1969), is new after the Council;[18] the book attempts to show the unity between the Council and the Church's tradition and lays down two conditions for genuine renewal: (1) a true love of Jesus Christ (taking position here against the popular forms of the Bultmannian

[17] Of course de Lubac had been familiar with this theme for a long time. See, for example, text 30 in the appendix to *Catholicisme* and the note in the same book at the end of chapter 6 (footnote 158). The theme reemerges in PME 100ff.

[18] There is no need here to go into the commentaries on conciliar texts, some of which are done in great detail, such as DV.

theology in vogue in France);[19] (2) a love concerned with ecclesial unity[20] (with Madeleine Delbrel as an illuminating example): a warning against one-sided theology, be it political or charismatic.

Paradoxe et mystère de l'Eglise (1967), a collection of articles, elucidates again the two title words and applies them to the Council that had just ended. The Church is paradox because she exists out of sheer contrasting aspects that cannot be conceptually synthesized and, precisely because of this, point to a mystery in which they are rooted.[21] But as mystery, she is greater than the believer who attempts to think her; he must rather thank her or—what amounts to the same thing—look upon her as his "mother".[22] Both as custodian of the word and the sacraments and as the one who gives birth to the saints, she always precedes the believing individual and prevents every form of human "self-adoration".[23] But insofar as she is mystery, no earthly concept can be adequately applied to her. This is true, to take but a few examples, of the concept of monarchy as applied to the papacy,[24] the concept of collegial-

---

[19] ECr 69ff. Barth (who is often cited in the latter work) is invoked as a counter-witness.

[20] ECr 85ff.

[21] PME 12.

[22] PME 14ff.

[23] PME 32ff.

[24] PME 39.

ity as applied to the unity of the bishops,[25] of both "people" and "body" as applied to the Church as a whole.[26] The antitheses in the Church remain irreducible. The article on "The Religions of Man According to the Fathers" makes an important contemporary application of the themes from *Catholicisme* and *Surnaturel*.[27] It is evident to the Fathers that every man is created according to the image of God, that Christ came to redeem all mankind, that, finally, the Church is called to make the whole world one in Christ. One hears in this the fundamental thesis of *Surnaturel*: "The image of God is imprinted in the depths of human nature and consequently in each man; this image is that something which constitutes in him—without his yet making any contribution to it—a secret call, as it were, to the object of the revelation, full and supernatural, brought by Jesus Christ."[28] Since the Church, even as visible, is essentially under way to the redemption of the world (the "kingdom"), the judgment of the Fathers upon the final destiny of the gentiles can only be a "dynamic" one.[29] All peoples are called to Christ and have (even according to Augustine) "their prophets", but it is impossible that their religions, considered as static systems (which,

[25] PME 41.
[26] PME 47.
[27] PME 120–67.
[28] PME 127.
[29] PME 129ff.

moreover, are in profound contradiction to one another), be accorded the value of ways of salvation ("ordinary" or "extraordinary") willed by God.[30] There is only one axis of world history, in which the truth of all religions is gathered and embodied.[31] If there can be men outside the Church who belong to Christ ("anonymous Christians"), still, in no way can there be an "anonymous Christianity",[32] as if the Church's only role in preaching were to bring to the light of reflection what was already present unreflectedly.[33]

Les Eglises particulières dans l'Eglise universelle (1971), which includes a second part on the motherhood of the Church, elucidates a specific postconciliar ecclesial problem that has already been mentioned: that of the theological relevance of the bishops' conferences, which had been given greater emphasis by the Council. In addition to mentioning the evident advantages, de Lubac also presents the limits and the dangers, prudently making the necessary qualifications, yet at the same time meeting the problem resolutely and directly: the intrusion of an anonymous bureaucratism[34] where theologically only the individual bishop has personally the full ecclesial (and collegial) responsibility for his

[30] PME 133ff.
[31] PME 141.
[32] PME 153.
[33] PME 149, and the appendix to B-W.
[34] EPU 227.

diocese (and therein also for the entire Church). The "conferences", which possess no legitimation from the original institution of the Church but (like patriarchates and the like) are secondary constructions, could theoretically and practically endanger the position and personal authority of each individual bishop. Against this, de Lubac emphatically directs a renewed attention to the ministry of Peter's successors for the unity and freedom of the Church.[35] There is an essential difference between decentralization and democratization.[36] The explication of the "motherhood of the Church" in the context of this work has a function other than in the earlier work. Here the fundamental thesis is that ecclesial authority can only preserve its necessary character of "fatherhood" (instead of "institution") where the motherhood of the Church is recognized and affirmed as the enveloping medium.[37] The appropriateness of celibacy is penetratingly discussed in relation to the Church's origin "from

[35] Chapters 6 and 7; noteworthy are the details on the method of electing the pope, EPU 127.

[36] EPU 132.

[37] On the enveloping motherhood and its paradoxes: EPU 167ff.; on the fatherhood of hierarchical authority: 157ff.; the necessity of authority for service and the determination of the limits of authority through the service of word and sacrament: 187; on fatherhood as the uniquely legitimate foundation of authority: 191f.; on the guarantee of the fatherhood of the hierarchical office by the motherhood of the Church: 288.

above" (in the Trinity).[38] In conclusion, the Church is presented as the only sanctuary of persons and personal values in today's anonymous mass society.[39] And this holds true, of course, precisely where ecclesial structure is centrally affirmed; on the margins of the Church, where conventicles begin, the personalizing force again becomes questionable.[40]

The work *La Foi chrétienne, Essai sur la structure du Symbole des apôtres* (1970) must also be considered in the cycle of the works thus far treated. For it is concerned not with a merely "Christian" faith but with an explicitly "ecclesial" faith (chapters 5 and 6); with the objective central mystery from which the Church—precisely through her faith—has a share in this mysterial character. After dismissing the naïve legend that the "twelve" articles of faith originated directly with the twelve apostles (chapter 1), the true tripartite structure of the *Credo* is demonstrated (chapter 2). It corresponds to the threefold question directed to the one to be baptized about his faith in God the Father, Son, and Spirit. But it is immediately shown (chapter 3) that the "*theologia*" (God himself) is and remains accessible only through the "*oikonomia*" (God for us in the life, suffering, and Resurrection of Jesus Christ); and it belongs to the *oikonomia* that Christ also is accessible in no other way than in and through the Church.

[38] EPU 198–209.
[39] EPU 219.
[40] EPU 225.

This elementary truth—though all too often forgotten in the scholastic treatises on the Trinity and Christology—determines de Lubac's theology throughout. In the following chapter, the uniqueness of the act of faith (conditioned by the object) is clearly brought out: "*credere in*" is a linguistic barbarism; it was formed to explain the dynamism of faith toward the God who is both absolute and personal. One not only *believes* the God who speaks; nor does one simply *believe in* God; but toward God, into God, as response to his self-surrender in his word.[41] The whole creature is caught up in this movement; it thus brings to its essential perfection the primordial movement of natural "religion", of the "*desiderium naturale*", of "piety"; and in this it also perfects the natural interpersonal act of holding-as-true the statement of another. Confrontation with the young Barth and with Bonhoeffer is necessary here.[42] Again the fundamental ideas of *Catholicisme* and *Surnaturel* provide the schemata for a fully Catholic understanding of faith (chapter 4). Proceeding along the lines of what had been said earlier, the fifth chapter establishes that the ultimate and complete subject of the Church's faith cannot be the individual but only the Church herself; and that there is therefore an education and initiation of the individual into this ecclesial act. If he be-

[41] FCh 164.
[42] FCh 172f., 182f.

gins by essentially believing the Church, in the sense of believing what she teaches, he ends by believing, "in and with" the Church, what she believes.[43] With this the initially predominant "obedience to the Church" is also transformed into a deeper obedience that, together with the Church and in her now-accepted Spirit, is exercised toward the Lord—an obedience that can be darker and more demanding than the earlier obedience (chapter 6). Now, at the high point of the inquiry (chapter 7), "the unity of faith" comes into focus: in content it is the faith in the triune God in his movement toward the world in the Christ event; in form it is the reception of this movement by the Church (dynamically taking the place of the world) that embraces in herself all individual acts of faith. Thus the *Credo* ultimately contains only a single dogma, whose mystery can and must spread out in many aspects. The perfect circle, however, already contains everything; it will not be enlarged or burst open through any new formulation.[44] Once again de Lubac comes to discuss the theme of "negative theology" and its ever-present impulse, which is already positive.[45] In the eighth chapter the historical dimension is treated: the breach in normal grammar (*credere in* . . .) is, like other linguistic irregularities, a sign of the crossing of the threshold from the customary old to the new,

[43] FCh 257ff.
[44] FCh 295.
[45] FCh 304ff.

for which no traditional word is adequate. And once again (chapter 9), this newness is not portrayed as intellectual and static but as a dynamic *"desiderium"* that finds rest in no finite reality. In the concluding (tenth) chapter, faith in God is seen in the world as a witness of one's existence, which is credible when it becomes an ever-deeper, interior union with the one believed in.

De Lubac's thought thus remains also, and precisely here, ecclesiocentric; he never conceives the content of faith (*theologia-oikonomia*) outside the point where it is found, within creation, unrestricted: in the Church's perfect act of faith, which is perfect in subjective holiness in the humble maid Mary; and is perfect in objective holiness in the authority of service instituted in her to guarantee the integrity of word and sacrament. God and world communicate here at the narrow passage of the hourglass, where the upper and lower vessels are open for each other. Every individual subject must therefore refer himself upward to this point in order to receive a share in the selflessness of the subjective-objective holiness of the Church, which alone makes possible the perfect reception of revelation and thus also the perfect orientation of the human *"desiderium"*. One could show that this center—a pure passageway for pure transmission of the gift—is also the center of the Ignatian spirit. Henry de Lubac lives so intimately in and from this spirit that he diffidently refrains from quoting the holy founder of the Society of Jesus among the thousands who throng his footnotes.

Like an unexpected variation toward the end of the symphony, more than four hundred pages are dedicated to Pico della Mirandola. Why Pico? Certainly not only because he was another great figure who needed to be vindicated of a thousand misinterpretations, restored from layer upon layer of paint, and given back to the great Christian tradition. And certainly not because Pico—who, dying young, was full more of promise than achievement and was entangled in many a contemporary academic wilderness before gradually freeing himself from all this—presents a rounded image of what de Lubac stands for. It is rather, on the contrary, because he so much points the way to greater openness of spirit and indeed with the same spiritual "independence",[46] the same instinct for the right direction that strives toward the universal, the catholic, as de Lubac himself.[47] When Pico focuses on freedom as man's innermost essence, he stands in the great tradition of Christian humanism beginning with the Fathers, yet he keeps an accent as personal as, for example, Teilhard had, when he spoke of the creature's élan toward God.[48] Imperceptibly, but unerringly, Pico goes his way, which leads him out of the closed sphere of the humanism of his time.

[46] Pic 284.
[47] Pic 80ff., 259.
[48] Pic 89.

He no longer understands the "*desiderium naturale*" naturalistically as Ficino did,[49] and man is more for him than a mere microcosm.[50] He gathers up all of tradition—even the four senses of Scripture[51]— elevating it in a "*Concordia*", a synthesis, a universal "*Pax*" that hovers before him but which he was only able to see and shape fragmentarily. He is akin to Cusanus in much that he says. How can the "*contradictoria in natura actuali*" be tolerated?[52] How can the great thinkers, Plato and Aristotle, be brought together in unity, not superficially, but profoundly (the theme of the treatise "*De Ente et Uno*", which de Lubac analyzes so illuminatingly)?[53] Pico knows, as does de Lubac, that all concepts and systems are indeed indispensable but limited; that their construction is due to a deeper force that also strives farther and beyond them. He combined this knowledge with a greater capacity for leadership than Erasmus, who shared this insight; how would it have been if he had lived long enough to en- counter Luther?[54] He sells his goods, as did Pascal, although he does not foresee his death; he dies in the

[49] Pic 74.

[50] Pic 160. Above all, man does not stand under the power of the stars; the treatise against astrology is another great testimony to what Pico means by freedom: 378.

[51] Pic 369–70.

[52] Pic 257.

[53] Pic 261–86.

[54] Pic 394ff.

arms of Savonarola. He unites in his brief existence the hunger to know, embrace and unify all with the calmness of one who knows how to be detached from everything. He unites both attributes, however, not in opposition to one another, but because he aspires to the greatest peace, that of all things being together in God. It all remains a torso, but one can surmise what was intended: perhaps, no, certainly more than what a man can attain on earth. And what remains of him, when his image has been purified, is the splendor that radiates from the *Imago Dei*, which lets him appear to the world around him as a kind of wonder, but one which ultimately shone before God and was known to God alone.

CONCLUSION

Everyone who watches fireworks expects the final burst of light to crown the show, to surpass the rest of the display in beauty, and to exceed our highest hopes. But who would have expected a finale of almost 1,000 pages from our eighty-year-old master, a new work with a broader intellectual scope than his others but judged at least their equal in detailed analysis and their superior in vigor? The public has yet to realize the greatness of the gift it received in the two giant volumes of *La Posterité spirituelle de Joachim de Flore* and to grasp fully how many doors it can open. In wonderment, we make our way through this forest of erudition, which leads us from Joachim himself to the "spirituals" and their tragic history, to Bonaventure and to Thomas, and slowly crosses the late Middle Ages to reach the mystic Cabalism of the Renaissance. From there it proceeds through Campanella, Bohme, secret societies, and the "Rose-Croix", finally to arrive at Pietism and the Enlightenment. Lessing and Herder are landmarks that point the way to German

The Conclusion has been translated by Susan Clements.

123

idealism, and soon a cast of very diverse individuals begins to make its appearance. We meet, among others, Saint-Simon and Michelet, Lamennais, Buchez, George Sand, and Mickiewicz, and encounter Marx as his movement takes root in the young Germany. In several of these individuals we mark an undisguised Joachimism. Hitler and the Third Reich are evoked; we are led across Russia from Tchaadaev to Dostoevsky, Soloviev, Berdiaev, and beyond; we encounter Ernst Bloch and Moltmann—to name just a few of the thousands of names that appear in this vast work.

Among them, we find a profusion of visionaries and dreamers whose theories and influence the author traces with as much care as those of the more important figures, who stand out immediately against this maze of names. But what good does this serve, this detailed work woven around a Calabrian abbot apparently lost in the darkness of time? Answer: The last work of Father de Lubac can be understood as the true conclusion to our last chapter on the Church. In the eyes of universal history, must the Church be understood as the next-to-last reality, the work of the second Person of the Trinity, just as creation and the Old Testament were the works of the first Person—a work that will be overtaken by an age of the Spirit, long-awaited, hoped for, and still to come? Or is she, as the one, holy Catholic and Apostolic Church, invested with the Spirit of the Father and the Son,

the final and definitive reality, filled with inter-
nal potentialities that will unfurl across the ages,
embracing them until the end? From within the
Church, Joachim called for her succession of herself into a new age—an age of the Spirit. Thus the
entire spiritual history of Europe can be read in
light of his thought: in a hundred different ways,
we have tried either to give the Spirit free reign
within the Church of Christ or to draw the Church
forcefully into a third age of the human spirit—
finally set free. These two lines of thought open
the way for myriad nuances and shades of difference. How many nuances appear between the two
extremes!—between, on the one hand, a Christian
attitude that sees the Crucified Christ as the ultimate manifestation of divine love, exhaling his
Spirit as a gift to the Church, and, on the other
hand, all the attempts, hesitant or more vigorous,
to push him beyond himself in some "theology of
hope"! Making our way through the thick of this
debate, we come to see that there is no other subject that is theologically more exciting or decisive
than this.

De Lubac exercises here, especially on the most
delicate points, his magistral art for the discernment of spirits. With passion we follow the author's description of Bonaventure, the Franciscan
General, as he attempts to lead the Joachimites of
his community back to the heart of orthodoxy
without disrupting the unity of his order; or again

the manner in which the author judges the very
definite Joachimite influence of George Sand on
Dostoevsky and describes how the great Russian
and his friend Soloviev, following in the path of
the Polish Mickiewicz, were finally freed from all
Joachimite influence. We must, however, leave
these details here to say in conclusion that Father
de Lubac, on the modest grounds of this work, has
uncovered and developed in all its depth and its entire extent the most pressing subject imaginable in
the spiritual history of the West. With an air verg-
ing on surprise, the conclusion of his work speaks
of "the strange fascination the Abbot of Flore continues to hold over the minds of today with his
archaic and yet extremely personal exegesis". This
should hardly surprise us, since finally this exegesis
evokes the apocalyptic battle that will decide if, in
reality, none other than the "lamb that was slain",
the lamp whose seven eyes are the seven spirits of
God sent to all parts of the world, will be worthy
and capable of breaking the seven seals of the book
containing the history of the world (Revelation 5).

Seeking to situate these two volumes within the
rest of Father de Lubac's work, we are surprised
to discover that they draw us back clearly to the
question of his first great work, *Catholicisme*. Just
as *Catholicisme* sought to open the Church beyond
her limited figure to God's entire salvation history
with the world, so too this last work demonstrates,
but from the opposite side, the Church's surpassing

of herself into the whole of history. *Catholicisme* made this self-surpassing—which is part of the essential structure of the Church—familiar to us; the Joachimite surpassing is thus superfluous in a reign of the Spirit, be it secular or sacred. The Church herself brings about this surpassing, and even more she coincides with it. No other idea than this can more vigorously display the organic unity of the life and work of Henri de Lubac.